INVESTING FOR KIDS

INVESTING
for kids

HOW TO SAVE, INVEST, AND GROW MONEY

DYLIN REDLING AND ALLISON TOM

ILLUSTRATIONS BY VERÓNICA GRECH

ROCKRIDGE
PRESS

Interior and Cover Designer: Elizabeth Zuhl
Art Producer: Sara Feinstein
Editor: Alyson Penn
Production Editor: Mia Moran
Illustrations © 2020 Verónica Grech
Author photo courtesy of © Monica May Design

ISBN: Print 978-1-64739-876-7 | eBook 978-1-64739-554-4
R0

For our parents, our wonderful family and friends, Lukey and Lele, and our 12-year-old selves who knew nothing about finances but were willing to work hard and enjoy the ride. A special shout-out to Allison's grandmother, who gave Allison her first piggy bank and taught her to save up for her first purchase (treating the entire family to the local ice-cream truck)!

Contents

How to Use This Book **viii**

How to Use This Book

I f you're interested in money—how to save it, how to invest it, and how to make more of it—then this is the book for you!

Here, you'll learn how to earn money, how to save money, and how to invest your money. We'll talk about the concepts of "risk" and "reward," and you'll discover why some investments earn more than others. We'll also discuss stocks and bonds, how you can invest in them, and how they can help you build your wealth. Lastly, you'll learn how to diversify your investments and, ultimately, how to make your money grow.

Along the way, you'll meet the Dollar Duo: Mr. Finance and Investing Woman. Mr. Finance can stretch his body almost as far as he can make his money last. Investing Woman can conjure up and multiply coins, jewels, and precious metals. The Dollar Duo will help explain concepts and guide you through fun games, quizzes, and interesting features about famous investors, historical facts, behind-the-scenes stories, and much more.

NOTE: Any word you see set in **bold** is defined in the Glossary at the back of the book so you can learn more about it.

When we were younger, we weren't taught about personal finances and investing. Our schools didn't offer classes like Money 101, so we had to learn about money either from our parents or on our own. Once we got older, we started to earn our own money by working at Internet companies such as eBay, StubHub, and Lumosity. During that time, we were able to save enough money to retire in our early 40s. (Most people aren't in a position to be able to retire until they are 65.) Now we run a website called RetireBy45.com to help other people retire early.

We'd like to share what we've learned with you. And here's a secret: The earlier you start investing your money, the more money you can make! Time is one of the most powerful tools for building wealth—we explain how this works in chapter 2, page 20—and as a kid, you have something that most grown-ups don't have . . . time!

Learning about money and investing is not only beneficial to you, but it can also be helpful to the adults in your life. So, have fun learning together! Just keep in mind that you should *never* invest your money without prior adult approval and supervision.

We hope that reading this book is your first step on an exciting journey that you can benefit from for the rest of your life.

Dylin Redling & Allison Tom
Founders of RetireBy45.com

THE DOLLAR DUO:
MR. FINANCE AND
INVESTING WOMAN

CHAPTER 1

Money 101

Money. We all spend it, but have you ever stopped to think about where it comes from or how we ended up with our monetary system in the first place?

In this chapter, we get to the bottom of it. We cover the basics of money and finance and answer many of the questions you may have, such as:

- Who invented money?
- How is money manufactured?
- How did we end up with our monetary system, anyway?

We'll also take a look at the very first coins and work our way up to virtual currencies such as Bitcoin. Then we'll discuss a topic everyone loves: how to make money! We'll consider a few jobs you can do to earn some pocket change. Then we'll look at how you might become an entrepreneur and start a small business. We'll also explore some different career paths you might choose as an adult. Most importantly, we'll talk about how to save all that money you just learned how to earn.

Money Doesn't Grow on Trees

We've all wasted money on something we didn't really want or need. Maybe it was an inexpensive toy that broke right after you brought it home. Or maybe it was a computer game that you desperately wanted and then rarely played. Perhaps it was a candy that looked good but tasted awful. The adult in your household probably responded by saying "Money doesn't grow on trees, you know!" You've heard that phrase many times, but where *does* money actually come from?

To really understand the answer to that question, we need a little history lesson. Thousands of years ago, people would *barter* for goods, which means they would trade one item of value for another item of similar value. For example, a farmer might exchange an animal (like a goat) for something they needed (like tools or clay pots). You can see that this may prove to be difficult after a while. (Imagine if you had to swap your comic books for your friend's bicycle. You would have to barter all your favorite comic books to get *one* bike!)

Soon, people started using *commodities* as a form of money. These were common items that most people needed and used regularly. Examples of commodities include spices, salt, and seeds. It was probably easier to purchase tools and supplies with a bag of seeds than with a goat. However, using commodities as money still wasn't ideal because seeds and spices could go bad and weren't always easy to transport. You can't carry around a 5-pound bag of salt in your wallet! That inspired people to think of other valuable items that could be treated as money, like precious metals.

Historians have traced the use of metal objects as money to as early as 5000 BCE. It wasn't until around 700 BCE that the kingdom of Lydia in Asia Minor became the first culture to make coins (see Historical Notes: "The History of Money" on page 6).

Eventually, other countries and civilizations began to make their own coins with specific values. Having coins with set values made it easier to exchange money for goods and services. This type of money was known as *representative money*, and it allowed governments and banks to value it with a specific amount of gold or silver.

Let's fast-forward to today. Most modern currency is no longer backed by gold or silver. Our money is now known as *fiat money*. (*Fiat* means "let it be done" in Latin.) This gives the government the formal authorization to state that the money has a certain value. In the United States, the Department of the Treasury is in charge of the production of money. Paper money is printed at the Bureau of Engraving and Printing (BEP), and the US Mint makes coins. The Mint even offers free tours of its Philadelphia and Denver facilities, which show how coins are made and the history of the Mint (see "In the Vault: The US Mint").

IN THE VAULT: THE US MINT

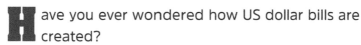

Have you ever wondered how US dollar bills are created?

The process has evolved quite a bit since their introduction in 1862. Back then, a small group of people used a hand-cranked machine to print money in the basement of the Treasury building. Today, the printing of money requires trained craftspeople, specialized equipment, and a combination of traditional printing techniques and modern technology.

Bills are made from a special blend of 75% cotton and 25% linen, with a security thread and watermark built into the paper. Designers develop the overall look, layout, and details using a combination of green, black, metallic, and color-shifting ink. A special print process called *intaglio* is used to add portraits, vignettes, numerals, and lettering for each denomination.

Afterward, serial numbers, the Federal Reserve seal, the Treasury seal, and Federal Reserve identification numbers are added. Computers, cameras, and sophisticated software thoroughly analyze and evaluate the bills before they get shrink-wrapped and delivered to the Federal Reserve System (the central banking system of the United States of America).

Ways to Earn Money

Now that you know where money comes from, let's talk about how you can start earning your own money.

You may be thinking, *I'm just a kid. What can I do to make money?* Well, there are many different ways you can earn some extra cash, even at your age. You just have to be a little creative and willing to put in the work.

Here are some things to ask yourself to help you get started:

1. **What do you enjoy doing?** Do you like animals? You could be a dog walker or a pet sitter. Do you like to be outside? You could mow lawns or do yard work. Do you like to ride your bike? You could run errands or make deliveries for people.
2. **What are you good at?** Are you good at art? You could paint fences. Are you good in the kitchen? You could bake cookies to sell. Are you good with younger kids? You could be a babysitter.

Remember to always check with an adult in your household to make sure it's okay for you to take on any job. Your health and safety always come first.

Once you're a little older, you can apply for a job where you receive a paycheck from an employer in exchange for your work. It feels very rewarding to get paid for a job well done. In fact, it's one of the first big steps to becoming an adult. (Note: According to the US Department of Labor, you can legally start working at the age of 14.)

One of my first jobs was making and delivering pizzas when I was 16. I loved driving and I loved pizza, so it was the perfect job for me! Allison's first job was cleaning CPR dummies when she was 17. It was messy work, but it paid well.

Another way people make money is by starting a business and becoming an entrepreneur. Did you know you can start a business without having any employees? It's called a *sole proprietorship*. Allison and I have started several of these small businesses.

HISTORICAL NOTES:
THE HISTORY OF MONEY

7th Century BCE:
The Lydian Empire became the first culture to make coins.

12th Century:
Paper money was introduced in China during the Song Dynasty.

1933:
The United States discontinued the gold standard to keep Americans from cashing in their currency for gold.

1913:
The United States established the Federal Reserve System.

1950:
The Diners Club Card became the world's first charge card.

1955:
The United States added the motto "In God We Trust" on all currency.

1958:
The BankAmericard was the first credit card issued by a third-party bank.

2020:
Over 5,000 cryptocurrencies are being traded.

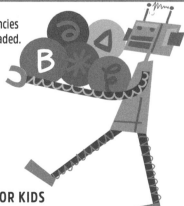

2014:
Apple Pay, a "digital wallet service," launched as a secure way to make payments via mobile (cell) phones.

1661:
The first European banknotes were issued in Sweden.

1792:
The US dollar was fixed to the price of gold and silver with the Coinage Act.

1816:
Gold was officially made the standard of value in England.

1900:
The United States enacted the Gold Standard Act, which led to the establishment of a central bank.

1872:
The first widely used service for wire transfers was launched by Western Union.

1862:
The first paper money was issued in the United States.

1967:
The first automated teller machine (ATM) debuted in London, England.

1990:
For the first time, all money transfers in the United States between its central bank and commercial banks were done in electronic form.

2009:
The cryptocurrency Bitcoin was invented by an anonymous person.

1997:
The first mobile purchase was a soft drink.

1994:
The first online purchase was a pepperoni and mushroom pizza from Pizza Hut.

MIX AND MATCH

The Dollar Duo wants you to brainstorm ways to earn money. Remember, a great way to do this is to think about what you enjoy doing as well as what you're good at to find the perfect job for you.

Make two lists: Write down five things you enjoy and five things you're good at. Then match them up to find your ideal job. Here's an example:

Things I like:	Things I'm good at:
swimming	helping people
comic books	art
board games	math

Now, look for ways to combine items from each column, like this:

swimming + helping people = swimming instructor

comic books + art = creating comics

board games + math = designing math-related games

You can use this strategy to brainstorm jobs you could do now as well as career ideas for when you're older.

BUG LIST

So, how might you decide on the type of business you should start? One trick is to come up with a "bug list," which is simply a list of things that bug you. Then think about what kind of product or service would solve that problem. Here are some examples:

⇨ **Problem:** You get fur all over you when you pet your cat. *Solution:* Invent a nonstick fur glove.

⇨ **Problem:** No superheroes look like you. *Solution:* Create a comic book with a superhero that inspires you.

⇨ **Problem:** Playing chess takes too long. *Solution:* Design a variation of chess that is less complicated.

You can also earn money by investing! We'll show you how to do that throughout this book.

Don't worry if earning money right now doesn't seem achievable. As you get older, you'll eventually find ways to earn an income. Meanwhile, the more you know now, the better position you'll be in to make money in the future.

What Is Debt?

The dictionary defines *debt* as "something, typically money, that is owed or due." Debt is usually incurred via a loan from a bank or financial institution.

Why would banks want to lend you money? They do it because they can charge interest (basically a fee) for that loan. Let's say Mary wants to buy a used car for $5,000, and her bank will lend her that money with 10% interest. "Interest" is an additional fee given for the delayed repayment of a debt. So, in one year, Mary will owe the bank

BUILD YOUR BUG LIST

In "Ways to Earn Money" (page 4), we talked about creating a list of things that annoy you—a bug list—and then creating a product or service to solve that problem.

For this activity, we want you to grab a piece of paper and a pen and write down 10 things that bug you. Beside each of those things, write down a possible solution.

Here are some types of things that might bug you:

food _____

clothing _____

cars _____

video games _____

bicycles _____

homework _____

restaurants _____

Don't worry if you don't come up with perfect solutions. The goal is to practice your problem-solving skills. You know what they say: Practice makes perfect!

$500 in interest (that's 10% of $5,000) in addition to the loan amount, making the total she will repay the bank after a year $5,500. The longer Mary takes to repay her debt, the more interest she will owe the bank.

While debt might sound like something bad, there is a difference between "good debt" and "bad debt." *Good debt* is used to invest in something that will increase in value. For example, a student loan, a mortgage, or a business loan. *Bad debt* is generally described as borrowing money at a high rate of interest for items that won't increase in value. High-interest car loans and credit card debt are some examples of bad debt.

Where to Keep Money

Let's pretend that you won $1 million in cash. Where in your home would you put it? Under your bed? In your closet? In a (very large) shoebox? Would you worry that your meddling big sister might find it or steal it from you? Or that your dog, Fluffy, might slobber all over it? Maybe you could stash it in a bunch of different places, but then you might forget where you put all of it.

This is exactly why we have banks and the banking system. Banks provide a safe place to store your extra cash, and they even pay you interest on your money! (We explained how interest works on page 9.) At your local bank, you can deposit your money into a savings account or a checking account, or you can buy **certificates of deposit (CDs)**. CDs offer higher interest rates, meaning they pay you more, but you have to let the bank keep your money for a longer period of time.

How do you know that your money is safe at the bank? What if there's a bank robbery and the thieves steal all the money? Or what if there's a fire and the bank burns down? Lucky for you, your money is safe because the Federal Deposit Insurance Corporation (FDIC) insures deposits up to $250,000. The FDIC was created in 1933 to provide stability in the financial system through the creation of safe banking practices. So, if you wanted your money to be totally secure, you could take that $1 million and deposit $250,000 in four different banks.

What do the banks do with your money? They lend it to other customers who are buying expensive things such as houses and cars. This sum of money that will have to be paid back with interest is called a *loan*. Banks are only required to keep 10% of cash deposits readily available. This regulation is called the *reserve requirement*. Banks lend out the other 90%, and they make money by charging higher interest rates on their loans than they pay for deposits.

This whole process helps the economy work more efficiently. People can use credit cards to make it easier to pay for everyday items. (Credit cards allow people to buy something now and pay for it later.) Borrowers can use bank loans for big purchases, like buying a house or paying for college tuition. Most people need a mortgage (a loan for a home) or some form of credit (the ability to borrow) to pay for these large items.

Where else can you keep your money? In addition to traditional banks, you can deposit it into Internet banks, **credit unions**, or **brokerage firms**.

- ⇨ **Internet banks** offer the same products and services as conventional banks, but they don't have physical locations. All of your deposits, withdrawals, and customer service inquiries are done online.
- ⇨ **Credit unions** are banks for specific groups of people, such as teachers or members of the military. They offer clients access to better rates, but they have fewer physical locations than most banks.
- ⇨ **Brokerage firms** allow people to buy and sell financial products such as stocks, bonds, mutual funds, and exchange-traded funds (ETFs).

Don't worry, we'll talk all about these exciting options in chapter 5.

If you don't have a bank account, ask an adult in your home if they can take you to their bank and help you open one.

FACE VALUE:
DEBBI FIELDS

Do you love chocolate chip cookies? This entrepreneur sure did!

At the age of 12, Debbi Fields became one of the first "ball girls" in Major League Baseball with the Oakland A's in 1968. She used her paycheck to buy ingredients to bake cookies, and she even created a "milk and cookies" break for the umpires.

"I knew I loved making cookies and every time I did, I made people happy. That was my business plan." Fields opened her first Mrs. Fields Original Cookies store in 1977 in Palo Alto, California. On her first day in business, no one came into her store, so Mrs. Fields took samples outside so that she could lure customers in to buy her cookies. Success! That day, she sold $75 worth of cookies (or more than $300 in today's dollars).

Known for warm, freshly baked cookies right out of the oven, Fields's secret was using real ingredients (butter, vanilla, and chocolate) to make her cookies. At one point, the Mrs. Fields company was worth $450 million. While Debbi Fields is no longer running the company, she still serves as a spokesperson for the brand, which has over 650 retail locations.

TAKING STOCK

In this chapter, we covered the basics of money and banking. Here are some things to remember:

☑ Bartering commodities was the very first type of payment (see page 2).

☑ The best way to earn money is to combine what you like to do and what you're good at (see page 5).

☑ Debt is money that is owed or due (see page 9).

☑ People put their money in banks because it's secure and they can earn money (interest) by doing so (see page 11).

Save
Your Money

When you get paid for walking your neighbor's dog or doing your chores, what do you do with the money? Do you immediately spend it on a new video game? Or do you try to keep some of it to use later? Spending is easy, but saving can be a lot harder.

In this chapter, we'll talk about the importance of saving your money and how much to save. You will learn about an amazing tool for growing your money called **interest**. And we'll show you why kids have an even more powerful tool for growing money than adults!

Spend or Save?

One of the most important money habits you can develop is learning how to save money. The sooner you start saving, the easier it becomes to save and grow your money. Most people think about saving for the future, but saving for the present is also important. The habit of saving helps you set aside money for things you might need or want to do, for emergencies, and for helping others.

One of the main reasons many people have trouble saving money is that they don't have a plan for savings. A good savings plan helps you figure out how much to save, how much to spend, and what to spend on. An example of a savings plan that you can use is called the *4-3-2-1 plan*. It divides your spending into four buckets:

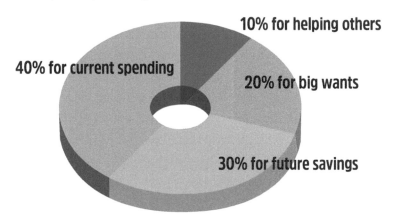

10% for helping others

40% for current spending

20% for big wants

30% for future savings

Let's look at what you might put into those four buckets:

⇨ **Current spending** would include smaller purchases (less than $50) that you make on a regular basis. Here are some examples: snacks, clothes, and doing things with your friends.

⇨ **Future savings** is money that you are saving for the future. This money could be used for college savings, your first car, and money that you want to invest.

◈ **Big wants** are larger purchases (more than $50) that you need time to save for. These could be things like a bicycle, video games, or a summer trip.
◈ **Helping others** is money that you could use to donate to charities, your community, and those in need. It could also be used to pitch in with your family and friends. Maybe you can buy a box of Girl Scout cookies from your sister or donate money to your best friend who is raising money for charity.

Now let's consider where to put your savings. In chapter 1, we talked about places people keep their money: traditional banks, online banks, credit unions, and brokerage firms. With so many options, how do you know where you should put *your* money?

There are two main types of savings: short-term savings and long-term savings.

◈ **Short-term savings** are there to help you pay for things you need on a regular basis. Your short-term savings would be for your "current spending" and "helping others" savings. This money should be easy to get to because you need it more often. You might start by keeping it in your bedroom in a piggy bank (where Allison kept her savings), a shoebox, or a small safe.
◈ **Long-term savings** are for things you will be spending on in the future, like a vacation or college. Your long-term savings are your "future savings" and your "big wants." Since you don't need this money right away, you can put it into a savings account or CD or invest in something like stocks and bonds. (We'll go over those later!)

Remember: You need an adult to help you put your money into any type of bank or savings account.

I t is a wonderful feeling to be able to help others in need. Being charitable can mean offering your time, resources, or money. It often starts with little acts of kindness, such as helping your little brother tie his shoes or setting the table for dinner. It also grows from gratitude. When you're thankful for all the things you have in life, it's easier to see those who are less fortunate.

So, what can you do? You can help others. You can contribute your time by volunteering at a pet shelter or a neighborhood cleanup effort. You can donate your old toys and clothes to a local charity. You can even give some of your money to causes you believe in, like protecting endangered wildlife, curing cancer, or ending hunger. (Just make sure you have an adult sign off on your plans first.)

Saving Money with Interest

One of the coolest parts about saving money is watching it grow without having to do anything. This is an example of what is referred to as **passive income**. You might be wondering, *How is it possible for money to grow on its own? It's not like a plant.*

The reason money can grow on its own is because banks pay interest on the money you deposit. They are actually paying *you* to keep your money with them. Why do they do this? As we mentioned in chapter 1, the banks lend out the money from these deposits and charge higher interest rates on their loans (see page 12).

There are two types of interest: *simple interest* and *compound interest*. Simple interest is very cool, but compound interest is even more amazing. The difference between the two is that simple interest is paid only on the amount deposited—this is called the **principal**. Compound interest, on the other hand, is paid on the principal *plus* accumulated interest from previous periods. (We'll explain that in the next section.)

Let's look at an example of simple interest in action. Let's say you deposited $1,000, and your bank offered to pay 5% simple interest per year. That means each year you would earn $50 ($1,000 × 0.05) in interest from your bank.

Here's how your money would grow over a 5-year period:

⇨ **Start:** $1,000
⇨ **After year 1:** $1,050
⇨ **After year 2:** $1,100
⇨ **After year 3:** $1,150
⇨ **After year 4:** $1,200
⇨ **After year 5:** $1,250

In 5 years, you will have earned an extra $250 on your $1,000 deposit *without having to do anything*. That's a total of 25% more money over 5 years ($250 ÷ $1,000 = 0.25).

This shows why it's important to start saving as early as possible. Remember when we said that kids actually have a more valuable tool for saving than adults do? That's right—that tool is *time*! You have the ability to let your money earn interest for many more years than adults.

For example, say you are currently 10 years old and your math teacher, Mrs. Smith, is 30 years old. If you both put $1,000 into a savings account today at 5% simple interest, here's how much you would each have when you are 35 years old:

⇨ **Mrs. Smith:** $1,250
⇨ **You:** $2,250

You would have $1,000 more than Mrs. Smith at the same age of 35! And this is *without* doing any more work for that money. Here's how it looks in a chart:

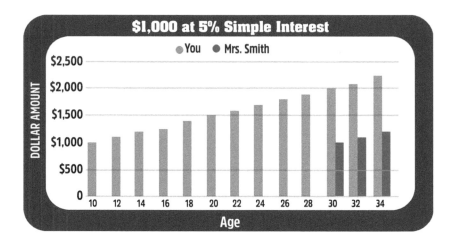

How did we calculate those numbers? There is actually a math formula to determine the amount of simple interest you would earn.

BE AN INTEREST RATE DETECTIVE

We've talked about all the different places you could put your money to earn interest, like your local bank and online banks. Some accounts will offer higher interest rates than others.

In this activity, the Dollar Duo is asking you to research the interest rates for the following types of accounts. Work with an adult on this and be sure to take notes so you can refer back to the information later.

⇨ **Local bank savings account:** Go to two or three local banks and ask them what their interest rate is for a savings account.

⇨ **Local bank certificates of deposit (CDs):** While you are at the bank, ask them how much interest they pay for 1-year, 3-year, and 5-year deposits.

⇨ **Online savings account:** Search for two or three online savings accounts and write down the interest rate they each pay.

Now that you have all of this information, you can decide which savings option would be best for you.

Simple interest = *P* × *i* × *n*

⇨ **P** = Principal (the amount you're starting with)
⇨ **i** = Interest rate
⇨ **n** = Term (how many years you're saving)

So, in the previous example with Mrs. Smith, here's how to calculate the amount of simple interest for both of you:

Mrs. Smith's simple interest = $1,000 × 0.05 × 5 years = $250

Your simple interest = $1,000 × 0.05 × 25 years = $1,250

Pretty cool, right? What's even cooler is *compound interest*, which we will explore next.

INSIDE THE VAULT: THE FEDERAL RESERVE

We talk a lot about interest in this chapter, but how is the rate of interest set, and how does it impact you?

The **Federal Reserve (Fed)** lowers interest rates when the economy is in a slump, and it raises interest rates when the economy is booming. The reason it lowers rates is to encourage people to borrow money. When the rates are lower, more people will buy homes with mortgages, cars with auto loans, and other goods with credit.

On the flip side, when interest rates go up, it's a good time to save your money. Higher interest rates will let you earn more money on your savings accounts and certificates of deposit (CDs).

Warren Buffett is one of the wealthiest and most well-known investors in the world. At the end of 2019, his net worth (the value of everything he owns minus what he owes others) was almost $90 billion!

Despite his wealth, Buffett lives by humble principles. He recommends investing in "simple businesses" that you can easily understand. He also suggests investing in index funds (see page 98) and not watching the markets too closely.

As a kid, Buffett went door-to-door selling chewing gum, bottles of soda, and magazines. In high school, he and a friend bought a used pinball machine for $25 and placed it in a barber shop. They added several more, and one year later they sold their small business for $1,200.

In 2009, Buffett founded the Giving Pledge with Bill Gates and has pledged to give away 99% of his wealth to charitable causes.

What Is Compound Interest?

We just showed why *simple interest* is so great for growing your money. You can watch your bank account increase without having to do a thing. Turns out it *is* actually like watching a plant grow!

The good news is that *compound interest* takes it up another notch. Warren Buffett, a billionaire and one of the world's most famous investors (see page 25), said this about compound interest:

"My wealth has come from a combination of living in America, some lucky genes, and compound interest."

So, why is compound interest better than simple interest? As we mentioned on page 21, simple interest is paid only on the principal, or the amount deposited. Compound interest, on the other hand, is paid on the principal *plus* accumulated interest from previous periods. This is what the formula looks like:

Compound interest = $P \times (1 + i)^n$

➡ **P** = Principal (the amount you're starting with)
➡ **i** = Interest rate
➡ **n** = Term (how many years you're saving)

Don't worry if this math equation looks too difficult. You can simply plug your numbers into an online calculator, like the one at Investor.gov. (You can find the link in the Resources section on page 127.)

Let's calculate compound interest using our previous example involving you and Mrs. Smith saving $1,000. With compound interest, here's how much you would each have when you were 35 years old:

➡ **Mrs. Smith:** $1,276
➡ **You:** $3,386

You would have $2,110 more than Mrs. Smith by the time you were at the same age of 35. *And this is without doing any more work for that money!* Here's how it looks in a graph:

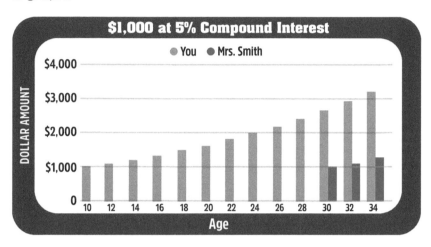

If you compare this chart with the one showing simple interest on page 22, do you notice anything different? *Hint:* Look at the blue lines in each chart.

If you look closely, you should be able to see that the blue lines in the compound interest chart slowly curve upward. The bars in the simple interest chart go up in a straight line. What this means is that the longer you invest your money, the more money you earn each year with compound interest.

Let's look at another example. What if you took that $1 million that you won in chapter 1 and invested it at 8% compound interest? In 25 years, you would have a total of $6,921,581! Your investment would have gone up more than six times without you having to lift a finger. It's almost like your money is your employee, and it's doing all the work for you.

So, how long does it take to double your investment with compound interest? The Rule of 72 says that to find the number of years required to double your money, you just divide the interest rate into 72. For example, at 8% interest, you can double your investment in 9 years (72 ÷ 8 = 9).

You can see why Albert Einstein, one of the most brilliant scientists in history, said this about compound interest:

"Compound interest is the eighth wonder of the world. He who understands it, earns it; he who doesn't, pays it."

DO THE MATH

In our examples comparing the rate of interest between you and Mrs. Smith (see pages 22 and 27), we used a 5% interest rate. But what if you could earn more interest than that? (We'll learn about higher rates of interest you can get at places called "the stock market" on page 68.)

The Dollar Duo wants you to calculate how much interest you would earn on your $1,000 over 25 years at *8% interest*. Try it with simple interest and with compound interest. As a reminder, here are the formulas:

Simple interest = $P \times i \times n$

Compound interest = $P \times (1 + i)^n$

⇨ **P** = Principal (the amount of money you're starting with)
⇨ **i** = Interest rate (the rate at which your money will grow)
⇨ **n** = Term (how many years you're saving)

And don't forget, you can use a compound interest calculator like the one at Investor.gov (see link in the Resources on page 127).

TAKING STOCK

In chapter 2, you learned about the wonderful world of saving money. Here are some things to remember:

☑ You can save with the 4-3-2-1 plan (see page 18).

☑ With interest, your money grows without you having to do anything (see page 21).

☑ Time is your best friend (which is why you'll have more money saved at age 35 than Mrs. Smith; see pages 22 and 27).

☑ Albert Einstein called compound interest "the eighth wonder of the world" (see page 28).

CHAPTER 3

Introduction to Investing

Y ou've learned about saving, and now we're going to take it to the next level and talk about **investing**. When you invest, you put money into something with the expectation that it will increase in value. Why is investing so important? You can't grow your money if you just stuff it under your mattress. Investing lets you use powerful tools like compound interest (see page 26) to increase your savings. (There's a reason the wealthiest people in the world are great investors.)

Investing can seem a little scary at first. How do you start? What do you invest in? Isn't it risky? We'll answer all of these questions so you can feel confident about the process. Once you understand the basics, investing won't seem nearly as scary anymore. Along the way, the Dollar Duo has some fun and interesting activities to help you understand and remember the concepts in this chapter.

Why Should You Invest?

Saving your money is great, but investing your money is even better!

Investing gives you a chance to earn even more than the interest rate the bank will give you. You can invest in a wide variety of financial products such as stocks, bonds, or a combination of these. You can also invest in physical things like real estate, art, or collectibles (like baseball cards).

Let's look at an example. A typical online savings account currently earns about 1.5% interest annually, but if you invested your money in the stock market (see page 68), the rate of return has gone up an average of almost 8% per year. If you had $1,000 to invest, your online savings account would earn $15 in one year. If you invested the same money in a stock, you'd earn $80 in that same year on your investment. That's a difference of $65! This is why investing is smart and not just for people with lots of money.

Why do investments earn more money than putting your money into a savings account? It comes down to something called "risk and reward." When you purchase stock in a company, you're taking a chance on that company. If it does well, then the stock will increase in value. If the company does poorly, then the stock value will go down. Fortunately, you can increase your odds of making good investments by doing research.

Let's look at the value of time in investing. In this example, you and Mrs. Smith will be investing and earning 8% interest per year. However, you will be starting much earlier than Mrs. Smith.

We'll also look at three scenarios:

1. You invest $1,000 per year for 10 years starting at age 15
2. You invest $1,000 per year for 10 years starting at age 25
3. Mrs. Smith invests $1,000 per year for 25 years starting at age 35

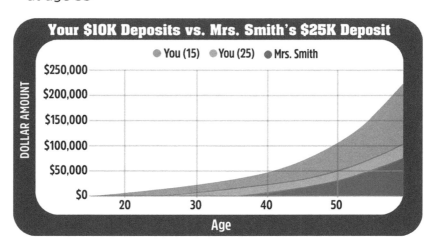

Your $10K Deposits vs. Mrs. Smith's $25K Deposit

Results at age 60:

1. Your total investment is $10,000, and you end up with $214,189!
2. Your total investment is $10,000, and you end up with $99,211.
3. Mrs. Smith's total investment is $25,000, and she ends up with $73,106.

Even though you invested $15,000 less than Mrs. Smith, you ended up with much more money at age 60. This is another illustration of the *value of time* for investing, which is an advantage you have over adults. The moral of the story is to start investing as early as possible!

Madam C. J. Walker (1867–1919) was an entrepreneur, philanthropist, and activist. You may have never heard of her, but her story is quite remarkable.

Walker was the first self-made female millionaire in the United States. (She's even in the *Guinness Book of World Records*.) She was also African American and the first child in her family born into freedom in the South.

Walker made her fortune by manufacturing and marketing cosmetics and hair-care products for Black women. She built a factory, hair salon, beauty school, and research laboratory at her company's headquarters in Indianapolis, Indiana.

During the 1910s, Walker's company employed thousands of salespeople, mostly women. In addition to training her employees on sales, she educated them about business, budgeting, and becoming financially independent. She was a true pioneer!

Risk versus Reward

How do you know what to invest in, and why do some investments do better than others? It's all based on the concept of *risk versus reward*.

Think of it this way: Your soccer coach decides she wants to be very aggressive, so she puts everyone (including the goalie) on offense. What would happen? Your team would probably score a lot of goals! But if the other team got the ball past your offense, they would have a free run at your goal. This is an example of *high risk, high reward*.

The following week, your coach decides to try a different approach. She puts every player on defense. The result would be the opposite. You would hardly ever score a goal, but you would also likely prevent your opponent from scoring. This is *low risk, low reward*.

Investing works the same way. If you invest in something that is risky, you might earn a lot more than other investments. However, the risk is that it could also go down in value more than those other investments.

The stock market is a good example. (We'll talk more about it on page 68.) Its rates have gone up on average about 8% per year. That is a great **return on investment (ROI)**, meaning that your investment made money, but remember that's the average. Some years it goes up much more than 8%, and other years the ROI can even be negative. You have to be willing to lose money occasionally in order to potentially achieve higher gains.

On the other hand, you could invest in something that has a much lower chance of declining in value, but your return on investment would be lower. A good example is your online savings account. The 1.5% interest won't go negative, but it won't go up much at all either. It gives you a low but steady return.

TO RISK OR NOT TO RISK?

How do you know how much risk you should take with your investments? Well, that depends on your comfort level in taking risks. Being *risk tolerant* means that you're okay with taking risks. Being *risk averse* means that you want to avoid anything risky. Several factors can help you when deciding on what level of risk you may want to take:

1. **Age:** When it comes to investments, the younger you are, the more risk you can take because you have *more time* to make up for it. If the rate of return on your investments goes down when you're 15 years old, you have decades to make your investments grow back before you retire.

2. **Your stage in life (which is similar to your age):** When you're a high-school student or get your first job, you can take on more risk because you have many years ahead of you to make up for any losses. But when you're an adult and getting close to retiring, you don't want to take big risks with your savings.

3. **Your personality:** Most people are naturally either risk averse or risk tolerant. Do you like adventurous things like skiing or surfing? Or do you think it's smarter to play things safe?

You have to be able to sleep at night not worrying about your investments. Knowing what kind of person you are— risk tolerant or risk averse—can help make decisions easier.

LIQUIDITY 101

When it comes to investing your money, another important thing to consider is **liquidity**. That's how easy it is to get to your money at any given time. If your money is tied up in something you can't access, then it's not liquid. For example, money in your piggy bank is liquid, which means that it's super easy to get to if you need it. Money that is invested in a special account for college isn't as liquid.

RISK OR REWARD?

Can you help the Dollar Duo come up with three examples of risk versus reward? You could use examples from sports, video games, or things outside your comfort zone (like giving a speech at school).

For each example, think about the following:

⇨ **What makes it high risk?**
⇨ **What could possibly go wrong?**
⇨ **What's the reward or win if you achieve your goal?**

Let's look at the previous soccer scenario as an example:

⇨ **What makes it high risk?** Putting all players on offense.
⇨ **What could possibly go wrong?** The other team could score because there's no goalie to block them.
⇨ **What's the reward or win if you achieve your goal?** Scoring many more goals.

Now come up with three different examples of your own.

If you have enough money available for the near future, then you can take more financial risks. If you need to have money available for immediate needs, you may want to play things safer. If there's an emergency, you want to be able to get to your money more easily.

HISTORICAL NOTES: THE GREAT RECESSION OF 2008

You may have heard people talk about the Great Recession of 2008. But what exactly was it, and what caused it?

In the mid-2000s, a lot of people were buying houses. To take advantage of the demand for housing, mortgage lenders—companies that lend people the money they need to buy houses—began loaning money to people who couldn't afford to pay them back. It had a domino effect. The mortgage lenders started going bankrupt because they weren't receiving the money they were owed on the poorly managed loans, and the housing markets began to collapse. Even large banks once considered "too big to fail" began to go under. All of this impacted the stock market, which lost about half its value.

Ultimately, the US government spent billions of dollars to save (bail out) several banks and struggling automakers. They then put financial regulations in place to protect consumers and prevent "predatory lending" to people who aren't financially savvy (unlike you). After reading this book, you will know more than most grown-ups!

RESEARCH, RESEARCH, RESEARCH

Okay, so now you are ready to invest. But how do you decide which investments make the most sense for you? Research. Plenty of research.

Let's look at an example. Imagine that three of your friends each want you to invest in their small business:

⇨ **Lilly washes cars.**
⇨ **Sophia has a lemonade stand.**
⇨ **Jack has a dog-walking business.**

The problem is that you only have enough money to invest in one of their businesses. You like all three of them equally as friends, so how do you decide which one you should invest in?

Asking the following questions is a great way to get started:

⇨ **What is your product or service?**
⇨ **How do you make money?**
⇨ **Who are your customers?**

Once you understand the goals of each business, it's time to delve deeper into the details. For each business you are considering investing in, you'll want to get the answers to even more questions:

⇨ **How much money do you earn?**
⇨ **How is your business growing?**
⇨ **Who is your competition?**
⇨ **How consistent is your business?**
⇨ **How do you manage your company?**

Let's look at each of these things in more detail; they're important factors in any business.

Earnings

A company's **earnings** (how much it makes) reflects its **profitability** or "bottom line." To determine how profitable a company is, you need to do a little math. Here's the equation you need:

Total income from sales – Total costs of running the business = Total earnings

Let's use Lilly's car wash business as an example.

Lilly charges $5 for every car she washes. In one weekend, Lilly typically washes 3 cars. She makes a total of $15. This is her total income for the weekend.

To operate her business, Lilly needs buckets, soap, and sponges. These items are her costs.

Lilly sometimes pays her little sister to help and also advertises her business by creating posters and posting them around her neighborhood. These are also her costs.

So, to know how profitable Lilly's business is, Lilly would need to tell you not just how much money she *earned* but also how much money she *spent* running her business.

Growth

In order for your investment to make money, a business needs to prosper or grow—it needs to make more money over time. So take a look at how much money each business has earned over the course of its life as a business. Can you see a trend? Is the business growing or shrinking?

Look at the company's earnings over the past few months to see whether they are going up or down. Remember that earnings will sometimes go down seasonally. For example, Sophia only sells lemonade in the summer. Look at a time frame that's big enough to give you a good sense of the overall direction that the company is going.

Competition

How many other businesses in the area offer the exact same or similar service? These are called competitors. Are there a lot of competitors? How does each business compare to one another? Is the company you are considering investing in a leader in the field? For example, are there other dog walkers in the neighborhood competing with Jack? If so, how does Jack make his service stand out? Maybe he charges less, or perhaps he walks fewer dogs at a time and gives each dog more time and attention.

Consistency

When looking at each company's numbers, check to see if they go up and down a lot. This indicates how consistent the business is. It's fun to go up and down on a roller coaster, but it's not fun to watch your money take a ride like that! Investors don't like uncertainty. One sign of a good investment is consistent and steady earnings over time that you can rely on.

Management

The most successful companies have excellent leaders. Great leaders have happier employees, make better product decisions, and create a positive long-term vision for the company. If you were to look at your three friends, which one would you trust the most to make the best decisions for their business? How smart, creative, and passionate are they?

DATA DUMP

The Dollar Duo is challenging you to choose three companies to research. The list could include your favorite companies or just companies that you're curious about.

Collect data for each of these criteria:

⇨ **Earnings:** How much did they earn last year?
⇨ **Growth:** Compare earnings from the previous year to the current one.
⇨ **Competition:** Who are their main competitors?
⇨ **Consistency:** Look at the pattern in their stock prices—do they go up and down like a roller coaster, or are they smooth and steady?
⇨ **Management:** Who is their CEO or chairperson of the board? Do they have a lot of experience in the industry? Are there any negative news stories about them?

After you do the research, decide which company you would be willing to invest in.

So, if you aren't friends with the person running the business you want to invest in, where do you get of all this information? You can start by doing an online search of the company name. Go to the company's website and look for any annual reports. You can also use investment tools from investment brokerage companies and get an adult to help you. Additionally, you can read about stocks on financial blogs and watch financial news programs on television.

Once you get used to doing this kind of research, you can do similar research for other types of investments, like bonds, mutual funds, and real estate. (We'll talk more about those later.)

. . . AND RESEARCH SOME MORE

Okay, you've done your research and decided on whom to invest in. You decide to go with Lilly's car-washing business. She's had steady growth over the past year, few competitors, and a creative plan to expand her business over the next year.

But wait! Just because you did all that research before you invested, that doesn't mean you're done. You should be continually tracking and monitoring your investment in order to manage it appropriately. Investing is an ongoing process.

Why do you have to keep watch over your investment? Well, what happens if things change for Lilly's car wash business? What if your other friend, James, decides he wants to compete with Lilly? He can charge less because he has more money to buy cheaper soap in bulk. He also has a little brother who will help for less money than Lilly's sister.

If James's business makes more sense for you, then you may need to make a change. It's important to always reevaluate your investments over time.

Make the World a Better Place

When you invest in a business, it's like becoming a part owner. So, you need to believe in the companies you invest in. In addition to looking at their performance, it's a good idea to also consider their approach to business, such as:

⇨ **Is their business working to make the world a better place?**

⇨ **Is the business "green"? Does it try to minimize pollution from its factories?**

⇨ **Does it sell products you are passionate about?**

Let's look at the three small businesses from the last section: Sophia's lemonade stand, Jack's dog-walking service, and Lilly's car wash. What questions might you ask to feel better about investing in each of them?

We'll start with Sophia's lemonade stand. Since childhood obesity has become a problem in our country, we could look at how healthy her product is. Does she use real lemons, or does she use a flavored drink mix with a lot of sugar and other unhealthy ingredients?

Next up is Jack's dog-walking service. Besides his earnings, what might influence you to invest with Jack? Perhaps if Jack gave a portion of his profits to a local animal shelter to support pet adoption, that might make his business more appealing.

And lastly, there's Lilly's car wash. Protecting the environment is very important, so we could look at how "green" her business is. Does she reduce water waste and use environmentally friendly soaps and sponges?

You can ask similar questions when doing your investment research. The concept of socially responsible investing (SRI) has become more popular recently, especially among younger investors. Here are some examples of industries that might help make the world better: affordable and clean energy, healthcare and medicine, fitness and nutrition, and education and the arts. To support gender and racial equality, you might look for companies run by underrepresented groups like women and people of color (e.g., Black, Hispanic, Asian, and Native American).

You may also want to avoid companies or industries that you consider harmful to the world. Examples could include tobacco, alcohol, gambling, firearms, and coal. It's important to use your judgment and invest in what you believe in. Just remember there's always a balance between "doing good" and performing well. Compare the socially responsible options with other companies in the industry when you do your research.

WHAT IS ESG?

One strategy to help you find companies that make the world better is called the *ESG method*. ESG stands for Environment, Social, and Governance. (You may have come across this acronym in your research.) Using the ESG strategy, you can identify companies that fall into one of the following categories:

E **Companies that are conscious about the environment.** This includes companies creating green products, reducing carbon footprint and emissions, and focusing on renewable energies (like solar and wind).

S **Companies that consider the social aspects of their business.** These companies focus on having a diverse workforce, valuing human rights, consumer protection, and animal welfare.

G **Companies that are well governed.** These companies focus on management and senior leadership and how well the company is run. This would involve things like communication with shareholders, making sure the executive team isn't overpaid, and ensuring that the workforce is fairly compensated.

Which factors are the most important? It's up to you to decide. Maybe you want to look for companies that are pioneering solar energy. Or, if you're an animal lover, you might look for companies devoted to animal welfare. Compare these companies with their competitors to make a final decision. And remember, it's important to continue evaluating your investments regularly.

YOUR MONEY'S WORTH: GOING GREEN

We all know that climate change is having an enormous effect on the world. One way to help is to consider the environment when choosing your investments.

Here are some green industries that are working on products to help the environment:

- ⇨ **Renewable energy: wind, solar, geothermal**
- ⇨ **Electric vehicles**
- ⇨ **Water and utility stocks**
- ⇨ **Waste reduction and recycling**
- ⇨ **Pollution control**
- ⇨ **Organic foods**

If you find the right companies and funds, you can make money while helping the environment at the same time!

PICK A STOCK, BUT NOT JUST ANY STOCK

The Dollar Duo is here to issue you a challenge. Which of the three companies you researched in the previous activity (see page 44) will perform best in the next month? Do you dare make a prediction? You can only choose one.

Base your choice on your research. This is a fun way to see how well your research works without actually investing real money!

Over the next four weeks, check each company's stock price each week (try to choose the same day every week) and record the results on a piece of paper, highlighting which you predict will be the "winner" (show the highest increase in performance).

You can make this an individual challenge, or you can invite others to play with you and see whose prediction increases the most!

TAKING STOCK

In chapter 3, you graduated from simply saving to learning about investing your money! Here are some things to remember:

- ☑ Investing can earn much more interest than a savings account (see page 37).

- ☑ Taking big investment risks is like having a soccer team that only plays offense (see page 36).

- ☑ It's important to research companies before you invest (just like you would before investing in your friend's lemonade stand; see page 41).

- ☑ ESG investing can help make the world a better place (see page 47).

CHAPTER 4

Low Risk/ Low Reward

Now that we've learned the fundamentals of investing, it's time to look at different types of investments as well as their level of risk. To help us, we'll rank each using our handy-dandy Risk-o-Meter! Each investment will get a risk rating from 1 (lowest risk) to 10 (highest risk). In this chapter, we'll focus on the low-risk/low-reward investments. (Chapter 5 will focus on high-risk/high-reward investments.)

The low-risk/low-reward investments in this chapter may not seem as exciting as higher-risk investments, but they have one big advantage: They basically guarantee that you'll get a return on your investment (it will just be a smaller one).

What kinds of investments fall into this category? These safer investments include Treasury bills, certificates of deposit (CDs), and different types of bonds.

Treasury Bills

Treasury bills (or T-bills) are one of the safest investments you can make because they are backed by the US Treasury Department. This means there is zero chance that the US government will *default* (not pay you back) on the T-bill. The US government guarantees repayment, so you know that you won't lose money on this investment. The downside is that the amount of return (or interest) is quite low.

You can purchase T-bills directly from the US Treasury online at TreasuryDirect.gov or through an investment brokerage firm. T-bills are typically sold in multiples of $100 or $1,000. This is called the *face value* (or sometimes the par value). When you buy a T-bill, you buy it for a certain period of time, which is called its **maturity**. The maturity time frames can vary from a few days to up to a year, but typically they are for 4, 8, 13, 26, or 52 weeks.

T-bills don't pay an interest rate like many other investments. Instead, you buy them at a purchase price and redeem them when they mature at their face value.

Here's an example of how it works: You buy a $1,000 (face value) T-bill for $995 (purchase price). When it reaches the maturity date, you get the face value of $1,000, so you made $5 on your investment ($1,000 - $995 = $5).

If you were to calculate the interest on that specific investment example, it would be 0.5% (interest rate = $5 ÷ $1,000). The amount you can earn on T-bills depends on the maturity date. The longer the maturity date, the more money you will make.

FACE VALUE:
STEPHEN CURRY

Most people know Stephen Curry as the point guard for the Golden State Warriors, where he has won multiple NBA championships and MVP trophies. He has revolutionized the game of basketball with his jaw-dropping 3-point shooting and elite ball-handling.

But did you know that Steph is also involved in business, philanthropy, and investments off the court? Curry partnered with Under Armour in 2013 and became the star of its footwear line. He also signed a film and TV deal with Sony Pictures in 2018, focusing on electronics, gaming, and virtual reality.

Steph has now teamed up with his former college roommate, Bryant Barr, on a company called SC30. The goal of this investment/venture company is to do three things: disrupt culture, transform lives, and "ruin the game" (being successful by doing things differently).

Curry's ultimate goal is to build something amazing that will be around long after his basketball career is over.

Bank Deposits and CDs

Next to T-bills, bank deposits (like savings accounts) and CDs (or certificates of deposit) are the next safest investments. The reason why bank deposits and CDs are so safe is because they are protected (up to $250,000 each) by the FDIC (see page 12).

Bank deposits fall into two categories:

1. Savings at a local bank (or credit union)

2. Savings in an online account

The advantage of savings at a local bank or credit union is that they have physical locations. Maybe you like to say hello to your local bank teller or get cash from the ATM. The disadvantage is that the interest rates are typically very low at a local bank. (In 2020, the average rate is 0.06%.)

Online savings accounts generally offer much higher interest rates (average 1% to 1.35% in 2020). The downside is that they don't have physical locations if you like to do banking in person. Fortunately, these days, everything can be done easily online. You can even connect your online savings with your regular bank account. With just a few clicks of your mouse, you can easily move money back and forth electronically.

CDs can earn slightly more interest than an online savings account (up to 2% in 2020) because you have to commit your money for a longer period of time. Just like T-bills, CDs have a maturity date (usually between 6 months and 5 years), and you earn more for longer time frames. But you have to be careful because if you take your money out before the maturity date, you'll have to pay a penalty.

What Is a Credit Rating?

You may have heard about credit ratings on television. It's like a score telling you how well or poorly something is performing. The higher your credit score, the more credit you can get and the better your interest rates will be. Like people, bonds also get a credit rating. Bonds can be issued by corporations or by the government (such as municipal bonds).

Bond credit ratings help show investors how risky it is to buy a particular bond. They provide valuable information about the issuer's financial situation. If you were a private investigator, these would be the clues you'd be looking for to see if the bond is a good or bad investment.

Think of it like a report card with letter grades. So AAA, AA, and A are the best ratings, with AAA being at the top (like getting an A+). These bonds are considered highly rated (or "investment grade"). Medium-risk bonds, called high yield, are rated BBB, BB, or B. And C, or lower, bonds are the riskiest (sometimes called speculative or "junk" bonds). Smart investors (like you) should steer clear of anything described as "junk"!

WHAT KIND OF INVESTOR ARE YOU?

What kind of Super Investor are you? Do you prefer low risk/low reward like Mr. Finance? Or high risk/high reward like The Investing Woman?

To find out, answer the following questions. Circle your answer—either a, b, or c. When you are done, add up the numbers in parentheses to determine your total score. Then check your score against the score card that follows to determine your investment style.

1. When you go to an amusement park, do you like riding the roller coasters?
A. No, thanks! (1)
B. Sure, if they're not too scary. (2)
C. Yes, the bigger and faster, the better! (3)

2. When you play sports, do you prefer offense or defense?
A. Defense all the way! (1)
B. A little bit of both. (2)
C. Offense. I love to score! (3)

3. You're at a pizza party. You can either get one slice right now or get two slices if you wait for everyone else to finish theirs first. What do you do?
A. Eat one slice now. (1)
B. Depends on how hungry I am. (2)
C. Wait for two slices. (3)

SCORE CARD

Let's see what your score says about your investment style:

⇨ **(3 to 4): Lower Risk:** You prefer a slow, steady, and safe approach. You don't mind waiting a little longer for your investments to grow.

⇨ **(5 to 7): Balanced:** You're in the middle. You might take some risks to grow your money, but you don't want to do anything that would rock your investment boat too much.

⇨ **(8 to 9): Higher Risk:** You are okay with a more aggressive investing approach. You're willing to take more chances with your money.

HISTORICAL NOTES: FINANCIAL BUBBLES

Let's talk about bubbles. No, not the ones in your bath! We're talking about *financial bubbles*. You know how bubbles work: When you blow a bubble, it starts small, then it gets bigger, and bigger, and bigger, and then . . . POP!

That's what happens with financial bubbles. It all starts with a new product, technology, or change in the market. Investors are curious and cautious at first, but then interest starts to build. Soon, people start to worry that they might miss out if they don't also invest in this **asset** (something of value). That's when people begin to feel euphoria (a state of intense excitement), and buying gets out of control.

Once everyone realizes the price of the asset has gotten much too high (from so many people buying it), we see a large and fast sell off. This causes the bubble to burst and sends the price of the asset plummeting.

Examples of financial bubbles are the Tulipmania in the 1600s (yes, it's hard to believe Dutch citizens were so excited about tulip bulbs), the dot-com bubble in 2001, and the Bitcoin bubble in 2018.

Highly Rated Corporate Bonds

Now let's take a closer look at bonds. When you purchase a bond, you're basically lending money to the bond issuer (a corporation or government) in exchange for some interest on that loan. You can also invest in a bond fund, which is a collection of bonds.

We will start with *highly rated corporate bonds*, which are low risk/low return. These bonds are also known as "investment-grade" bonds. They have credit ratings of BBB or higher (see "What Is a Credit Rating?" on page 57).

The high credit ratings for these bonds mean that the issuer is in good financial shape and most likely will not *default*, which is when the corporation issuing the bond cannot pay back its debts. Usually defaulting means the corporation is headed toward **bankruptcy**. If you were investing in a bond that defaulted, you might only get a portion of your money back.

The good news is that highly rated corporate bonds are a very safe investment. To illustrate how safe these bonds are, less than 1% of AAA bonds defaulted from 1920 to 2009. Of course, the downside to a safe (or low-risk) investment is that the return is also low. With bonds, the return is called the **yield**. Investors accept a lower yield on highly rated bonds in exchange for having a safe place to invest their money.

SEARCHING FOR BONDS

Now that you know about investing in bonds, can you help the Dollar Duo do some research? They would like to invest in bond funds, which is a group of bonds. Buying bond funds is an easy way to try bond investing.

When you search for bond funds (for example, you can type "bond funds California" into a search engine), you will get many results. You can click on a site such as Morningstar.com and look for the following types of information:

⇨ **Yield or Interest Rate:** The rate of return for this investment
⇨ **Expense Ratio:** How much it costs to manage the fund
⇨ **Inception Date:** How long this fund has been in existence

Note: To get a true rate of return, you'll want to subtract the **expense ratio** from the yield (or interest rate). This is important so that you can compare it with investments that don't have expense ratios.

You're looking for a good overall return (rates will vary, but look for 3% to 5% as a starting point) as well as a fund that has been around for a while. If it's a brand-new fund, you can't see how well it has performed over time.

Find three bond funds that look like interesting investments for the Dollar Duo.

High-Yield Bonds

Now we'll look at bonds that have a higher risk and reward. These are called *high-yield bonds*. Can you guess why? Of course, it's because they typically offer a higher yield (or rate of return)! However, as you now know, greater potential reward also means there's more risk involved. These bonds are also called "non-investment grade" or even "junk" bonds (not a great name, right?).

On the credit-rating scale (see page 57), high-yield bonds would be those rated BB or lower. Remember that a BB rating is like getting a B (or worse) grade on your report card. So, why would you invest in a bond that isn't at the top of its class? These bonds pay a higher yield as an incentive for the investor who is willing to take a risk on them.

Just be careful: You don't want to invest in a bond that has too low of a credit rating. Typically BB, B, or even CCC ratings indicate that the corporation can pay its debts. However, corporations with a CC or lower rating are much more likely to default.

It works the same way for consumers. If you were applying for a loan (or a credit card) from your bank, it would look at your credit report. The bank would then check your *credit score*. A good score means you're likely to pay your debts, so the bank will charge you a lower interest rate. A bad score means you will have to pay a higher interest rate because the bank is taking a risk lending to you.

IN THE VAULT:
RISING STARS AND FALLING ANGELS

High-yield bonds (BB rating or lower) have two subcategories with very interesting names: *rising stars* and *falling angels*.

Rising stars are bonds that currently have a low credit rating, but their financial situation is improving. Many times, these are newer companies that don't have much of a financial track record yet. They have to prove themselves before officially getting that better credit rating.

Falling angels are going the opposite way. These are companies whose credit rating has been downgraded. Usually this is due to a reduction in **revenue**. If the company is not bringing in as much money, then it will probably have a harder time paying its debts.

TAKING STOCK

In chapter 4, we talked about actual investments! Here are some things to remember about these "low-risk/low-reward" options:

☑ Treasury bills are the least risky investment because they're backed by the US government (see page 54).

☑ You can set up a savings account or buy a CD at your local bank or through an online bank (see page 56).

☑ A bond has a credit rating that's just like a grade on your report card. A highly rated bond is lower risk, lower reward, while a high-yield bond has higher risk with higher reward (see page 61).

CHAPTER 5

High Risk/ High Reward

I n this chapter, we're going to switch gears from low-risk/ low-reward investment types to high-risk/high-reward investment types. Low-risk/low-reward investments are kind of like riding a bicycle slowly along a flat street. Think of high-risk/high-reward investments like driving in a sports car around windy cliffside roads. You'll be in for a thrilling ride, but if you're not careful, you might drive off the cliff (financially, of course)!

We will talk a lot about the stock market in this chapter: how to buy stocks, what dividends are, and the difference between a recession and a depression. We'll also learn about *bulls*, *bears*, and *black swans* (not the ones at the zoo!). You'll find out what these three animals have to do with the stock market.

Stocks may seem scary to anyone who has never invested in them (they're even scary to some people who *have* bought them!), so we'll make sure you really understand them. And stocks aren't even the riskiest investment you can make. We'll talk about three investments with an even higher risk and reward!

The Stock Market

What do you think of when you think of the *stock market*? Maybe it's Wall Street with people in business suits rushing around like you see in the movies. Or you may think of the New York Stock Exchange, with stock prices flashing on large screens and people screaming, "Buy! Buy! BUY!"

The stock market started out like a grocery store where you could buy and sell stocks in person. (Now it can be done electronically.) There are three major stock markets in the United States alone. The largest is the New York Stock Exchange (NYSE), followed by the Nasdaq (pronounced *naz-dak*) and the American Stock Exchange (AMEX). There are also different stock exchanges around the world, such as the *Tokyo Stock Exchange* and the *London Stock Exchange*.

These stock markets consist of companies that are *publicly traded*—that means individual investors (like you or me) can buy **stock shares** of that company. By buying shares of a company, you are becoming a partial owner in that company. When the company does well, its stock price goes up, and your investment also goes up. However, when the company does poorly, its stock price goes down, and your investment goes down as well. This is why doing your research is so important (see page 41)!

You may have also heard of the Dow Jones and the S&P 500. These are examples of **stock indexes**. Stock indexes are a smaller part of the overall stock market. The Dow Jones Industrial Average (DJIA), sometimes just called *the Dow*, follows 30 of the largest US stocks. And the S&P 500 tracks the largest 500 stocks. There are many other indexes, but these are the most common. Sometimes investors will refer to these indexes to get a sense of the overall trends in the market. They may say, "The Dow is up 100 points today!"

How can you get started investing in the stock market? How do you actually buy stocks? Well, there are a couple of ways you can do it:

1. You can buy shares in an individual company, like your favorite entertainment or food company. The company will have a symbol associated with it, called a *stock ticker symbol,* which allows you to look up that specific company to do research or purchase it.
2. You can buy groups of stocks, called mutual funds or ETFs (exchange-traded funds). This allows you to create what's called a *diversified portfolio.* (We'll talk more about diversification later in this chapter.)

It helps reduce your risk if you own a number of different stocks (and other investments) because if one goes down, then another one may go up, and you don't end up losing everything.

GAMBLING AND LOTTERIES

You might think that gambling or playing the lottery is like investing. You put money in, and you hope that you win and get more money back. Sounds pretty simple, right? Not so fast!

Today, the odds of winning Powerball is *1 in 292.2 million,* and the odds of winning Mega Millions is *1 in 302.6 million!* Do you know what has better odds? All of these things:

- ⮑ **Being killed by a hippopotamus:** 1 in 2.5 million
- ⮑ **Becoming an astronaut:** 1 in 12.1 million
- ⮑ **Becoming president of the United States:** 1 in 32.6 million
- ⮑ **Being killed by a falling coconut:** 1 in 50.7 million

If you think gambling is any better, just remember that the casino always gives itself better odds than you. (That's how it makes money.)

You're much better off doing your research and making educated investments. After you finish reading this book, you will know how to make intelligent investments that will be profitable over time. One statistic that you may like is that about 1 in 30 Americans is a millionaire. Very few of them got there by gambling!

BEARS, BULLS, AND BLACK SWANS

If you've ever seen *The Wizard of Oz*, then you'll remember Dorothy and her friends singing about "lions and tigers and bears, oh my!" Well, in the investment world, the animals would be bulls, bears, and, in some cases, black swans.

There's a famous statue of a bull on Wall Street. Know why? A "bull market" means the stock market is going up (because a bull attacks its enemies by waving its horns upward). So the bull is considered to be a positive symbol. On the other hand, a "bear market" means that the stock market is going down (because most bears swipe their sharp claws down on their prey)—not so great.

A bull market is when the stock market *goes up* by 20% or more for at least 3 months. A bear market is when the stock market *goes down* by 20% or more for at least 3 months. Sometimes investors will just say that the market is "bullish" or "bearish" to describe the general trend of the stock market.

The good news is that there have been many more bull markets than bear markets throughout history. In fact, from 1926 to 2018, the average bull market lasted 9.1 years and the average bear market lasted only 1.4 years. In addition, the average *cumulative total returns* for the bull markets were a whopping 480%, while it was only -41% for the bear markets. So what does it all mean? Long story short, the stock market goes up much more than it goes down.

Another animal that is sometimes associated with the financial world and the stock market is a *black swan*. As you know, most swans are white, so seeing a black swan is considered a rare event. In economics, a *black swan event* describes something that rarely occurs, is completely unexpected, and has very negative consequences.

Some recent examples of black swan events were the dot-com bubble of 2001, the housing market crash of 2008 (see "Historical Notes: The Great Recession of 2008" on page 40), and the COVID-19 (or *coronavirus*) pandemic of 2020. In fact, the COVID-19 pandemic is probably the best example of a black swan event. It was an extremely rare event (the last major pandemic was in 1918), it had catastrophic financial effects (sharp declines in the stock market and massive unemployment), and it was completely unexpected.

It's impossible to predict black swan events before they happen, but we can use them as learning experiences. As an investor, you can make sure you do your homework and create your investing strategy. Do you remember when we talked about bubbles (see page 60)? You can make sure you don't get carried away in the excitement of a bubble. You can also diversify your investments. (We will talk all about *diversification* in the next chapter.)

FACE VALUE: BARBARA CORCORAN

Barbara Corcoran is a businessperson, investor, and writer. She has a net worth of $80 million! If you have ever watched the popular TV show *Shark Tank*, then you've probably seen her in action doing deals alongside other investors like Mark Cuban and Kevin O'Leary.

Some of Barbara's biggest deals on the show were for Coverplay (slipcovers for children's play yards), LOLIWARE (compostable and edible cups), and Stress Free Kids (books to help kids find inner peace).

In the 1970s after working as a receptionist for a real estate company, Barbara decided to start her own business. She founded her own real estate firm called The Corcoran Group. In 2001, Barbara sold her business for $66 million!

RECESSIONS VERSUS DEPRESSIONS

A *recession* is defined as a period of significant widespread economic decline that lasts more than a few months. That's quite a mouthful! In other words, the **gross domestic product (GDP)**, which measures all of the products and services created in the economy, has continued to go down over at least a few months. This means that people are buying fewer products, factories are producing less, and retail stores are selling fewer items.

What causes a recession? We have already talked about two of the major causes: financial bubbles and black swan events. The dot-com bubble in the early 2000s and the housing bubble in 2008 caused recessions. The coronavirus outbreak caused a recession in 2020. Other possible causes are an economic shock (like rising oil prices) or rising interest rates, which make borrowing too expensive.

A *depression*, on the other hand, is a more severe recession that lasts for years. The Great Depression has been the United States' only depression so far. (Fingers crossed that it stays that way!)

The good news is that recessions and even depressions are temporary. They're painful when they're happening, but eventually the markets rebound. This up-and-down flow is part of the overall economic process. Good investors are able to ride out the bear markets and recessions because they know there will be even longer bull markets afterward.

The chart that follows shows the Dow Jones Industrial Average (DJIA) from 2000 to 2018. You can see when the two recessions occurred where the line goes down for several months: the dot-com bubble in the early 2000s and the Great Recession from 2008 to 2009. Fortunately, you can also see that the markets have been able to recover after each recession.

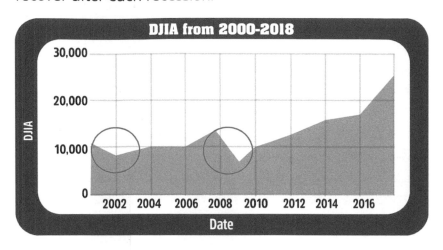

DJIA from 2000-2018

HISTORICAL NOTES:
THE GREAT DEPRESSION

You may have heard some, well, depressing things about the Great Depression, but what was it?

On October 29, 1929 (aka "Black Tuesday"), the American stock market (see page 68) collapsed. Stocks had become highly overvalued after years of wild speculation during the Roaring Twenties. This led to a panic by customers who tried to sell all their investments at once. Investors lost billions of dollars, and by 1933 more than 15 million Americans were unemployed and nearly half of the country's banks had failed.

In 1933, President Franklin D. Roosevelt signed the Banking Act of 1933 (also known as the the Glass-Steagall Act) into law. It was part of the president's New Deal, a series of federal relief programs and financial reforms to pull the United States out of the Great Depression. This legislation also established the Federal Deposit Insurance Corporation (FDIC), which is a government office that provides protection to people who deposit their money into banks.

HOW TO BUY STOCKS

Before the Internet, it was a lot harder to invest in **stocks**. You had to do your research in the library or by reading financial newspapers (like the *Wall Street Journal*). Once you decided what you wanted to buy (or sell), you would call your stockbroker (someone who buys and sells stocks). You would let them know which stocks you wanted to buy (or sell), and then they would put the order in for you. *Whew, that's a lot of work!*

Fortunately, It's much easier now that we have the Internet. You can do all the buying, selling, and research yourself right online. Here are the four steps to buy your first stocks (just make sure you have an adult help you throughout the process):

1. **Open an online account.** You will want to set up an account at an online brokerage or a mobile app. There are many options, so do a little research to see which ones are best for new investors. Some brokerage examples are Vanguard, Fidelity, and Charles Schwab, or you could look at apps such as Stockpile or Robinhood.

TO THE FUTURE!

When the Dollar Duo invests for the future, they find it helpful to think about how businesses and industries might evolve over time.

For example, in 1990—only 30 years before this book was written—there were no Wi-Fi, no text messages, and no electric cars. (That probably sounds like we lived in caves with dinosaurs outside to you!). In 2020, we see those products everywhere.

Help the Dollar Duo think about what businesses and products might be like 30 years from now in the following industries. Will anything be the same, or will everything be completely different?

⇨ **Transportation**
⇨ **Travel**
⇨ **Healthcare**
⇨ **Real estate**
⇨ **Food**

This exercise will help you think about which companies and industries make sense to invest in for future growth.

You will then be able to connect your regular bank account to your brokerage account.

2. **Select stocks.** Remember to do your homework! You can do a lot of the research right on the brokerage website. Just search for the stocks you're interested in and follow the steps from the research section of this book (see pages 41 to 45). Note: You can also buy groups of stocks, called mutual funds or exchange-traded funds (ETFs). (We'll talk about those in the next chapter.)

3. **Decide how many shares you want.** You can purchase a certain number of shares, or you can buy by the dollar amount. For example, let's say you want to invest up to $250. The stock you would like to buy is $100 per share. You could select two shares, which would cost you $200. Or you could select to buy $250 worth of the stock, which would give you 2.5 shares.

4. **Select the order type.** When buying stock, there are several different types of orders you can make. The two most common are *market orders* and *limit orders*. A market order is simply buying the stock at whatever the current price is. If the current price is $27, then you would pay $27 per share. With a limit order, you can decide what price you would prefer to pay for the stock. In this example, if you thought the price might come down, you could put in a limit order to buy at $25. This way the purchase wouldn't happen unless the price went down.

That's not too difficult, is it? For many people, buying stocks can seem scary. But once you know how it works, it's pretty easy!

The next part is to keep track of your stocks. Remember when we talked about research and investing in your friend's small business? We said you should keep track of their business to make sure it's still a smart investment. Buying stocks works the same way. You want to keep an eye on the companies you're investing with to make sure they continue to perform well.

DIVIDENDS

Next up we get to the good stuff: how to *make money* with stocks. There are two ways:

1. **The price of the stock goes up.** Let's say you bought 10 shares of a stock for $15 per share. That's an investment of $150 (10 shares × $15). If the price of that stock goes up to $20 per share next month, then your investment is now worth $200 (10 shares × $20). You just made $50!

2. **Investing in stocks that pay dividends.** Many companies will give investors a portion of their earnings to reward them for being shareholders. It can be in the form of either cash or additional shares of stock. This is called a dividend. In fact, some companies even pay dividends when they don't have positive earnings. Why would they do that? They may have a long record of offering dividends, so they want to continue that tradition. Companies that pay dividends tend to be larger, more established institutions.

When you're researching which stocks to buy, check to see if they pay dividends. Getting dividend payments is a great way to ensure that you get a regular return on your investment (even when the stock price is fluctuating or going down). However, don't make dividends your only reason for picking a stock. You want to make sure it meets the other criteria from your research list, too (strong earnings, growth, stability, etc.).

PICK THREE

The Dollar Duo wants you to find three investment brokerages you might consider using.

There are many different kinds. In the 1970s and 1980s, a number of low-cost investment brokerages became popular. These include firms like Vanguard, Charles Schwab, and Fidelity. In the 2000s, online investment brokerages started to spring up, such as E-Trade, TD Ameritrade, and Robinhood. And now there are even companies that offer robo-advisors, which are automated software platforms that make many of the investment decisions for you. Look around and find three firms you think you would consider using.

When doing your research, make notes on things like fees, commissions, minimum balances, and security (like the use of *two-factor authentication*, which requires a code from your mobile phone). As a new investor, low minimum balances and low fees are important. However, lower fees and commissions usually mean that you have to make more investment decisions on your own (instead of with a financial advisor).

BUY LOW, SELL HIGH

There is a saying in the investing world that you should "*buy low, sell high*." This is great advice, but it's easier said than done. Psychology and emotion play a big part in people's decisions.

For example, when the market is going up, people get excited and say, "Wow, look how great the stock market is. I better buy!" So they buy when the price is higher. When the market is going down, people get scared and say, "I better sell and get out now while I can!" And they sell when the price is lower.

How do you avoid this? Try to make your decisions based on your research and be patient. Remember: You have time on your side. Smart investors look way into the future. Remember the graph of the bear markets on page 74? The markets always came back afterward. If you sold your stocks during those down times, you would have lost money. If you held them, you would have made much more.

Private Equity

You now know that when you invest in the stock market, you are purchasing shares in publicly traded companies. These are companies that exist on the NYSE, the Nasdaq, or other stock exchanges.

But what about companies that are not on the stock market? Believe it or not, only 1% of all companies in the United States are publicly traded. That means the vast majority of businesses are *privately held*. These include the small businesses in your neighborhood, like the bowling alley, the dry cleaner, and the doctor's office. It also includes larger companies that prefer to remain privately held (so they don't have to disclose their finances to the public) plus growing companies that hope to be public someday through a process called an *initial public offering* (IPO).

So, is it possible to invest in these private companies? You bet, through an investment called *private equity*, which allows some investors to own a portion of a private company. However, only certain types of investors can qualify to invest in private equity. Examples would be insurance companies, pension funds, foundations, and very wealthy individuals. The reason only very wealthy individuals can invest in private equity is because the minimum investments are very high. Some funds require as much as $250,000 and others over $1 million!

Although you may never invest directly in private equity, it is possible that you might invest indirectly if you ever participate in a *pension plan* (receiving money from your employer when you retire) or own an insurance policy. Many of those companies invest a portion of their holdings in private equity funds.

YOUR MONEY'S WORTH: DIVERSITY

When deciding which companies to invest in, you might consider looking at companies with diverse ownership. Women and people of color often face discrimination and unfair treatment in the workplace and business community, so this can be your chance to give back.

Minority-owned businesses are companies that are owned by at least 51% of a minority group such as Asian, Black, Hispanic, or Native American. One resource is the Minority Business Development Agency (MBDA), which helps support the growth and development of minority-owned businesses.

You may also wish to support women-owned companies. Many women find it harder to start businesses due to social and cultural biases, family and child-rearing obligations, and lack of educational and community support. The US Women's Chamber of Commerce is one organization dedicated to helping women business owners.

To find businesses to invest in, search for "minority-owned businesses" or "women-owned businesses" using your favorite search engine.

RISK-O-METER

Venture Capital

Another type of investment in the private sector is called *venture capital*. The word *venture* means "a risky or daring undertaking." Based on that definition, you can probably imagine that venture capital investments are riskier than most other forms of investing. These investors are taking a chance on new emerging companies (see "What's a Startup?" on page 86), whose financials and business models are still in their early stages.

Venture capital investments can come from a venture capital firm (also called a VC) or from high-net-worth individuals. The investments are usually in cash, but they can also be investments in the form of knowledge and expertise. Many times the VCs will get a seat on the board of directors of the startups they invest in so that they can provide guidance to the young company.

If venture capital investments are so risky, why does anyone do them? It all goes back to the rule of high risk, high reward (see page 37). The risks are higher than most investments, but the potential rewards are also higher. Many of the startups that VCs invest in are run by younger, less experienced entrepreneurs. They also may be selling a new product or service that nobody has seen before. If it does well, then the investors win big. But if it fails, then a lot of money and time are lost.

Many popular technology companies were helped in their early stages by venture capital: Facebook, WhatsApp, Twitter, and Google, to name a few. But for every successful VC-backed company, there are many that flop.

IN THE VAULT: TAKING IT PUBLIC

When a company "goes public" with an IPO, it's a really big deal. An IPO transforms a private company into a public company, which allows it to raise money for expansion and become publicly traded on the stock market.

The company founder may start it off by ringing the bell at the New York Stock Exchange (NYSE). You have to ring it for at least 10 seconds, or else the traders on the floor will boo at you.

TO INVEST OR NOT TO INVEST

Let's play a little game. Help the Dollar Duo decide which of the following business ideas they should invest in. Answer *yes* or *no* to each of the following ideas. (These ideas are from real companies that either did well or went out of business.)

1. A juicer connected to Wi-Fi
2. Sauce holders for your car
3. A system for ranking people's social influence
4. A padlock that opens with your fingerprint
5. A night light for your toilet
6. A search engine for apps

   Based on these product descriptions, which businesses would you recommend that the Dollar Duo invest in? When you're finished, check the answer key to see the names of these real businesses.

Answer Key

Here are the actual businesses and whether they succeeded:

1. Juicero—failed
2. Saucemoto—successful
3. Klout—failed
4. BenjiLock—successful
5. IllumiBowl—successful
6. Quixey—failed

The NYSE prepares well in advance to make sure everything runs smoothly. The night before, analysts, called *underwriters*, determine a price for the new stock. Once the stock is added to the exchange, it takes, on average, over 10 minutes for the price to settle in on a number. When everyone is satisfied that the price has been set, a second bell is rung with a ceremonial gavel. At that point, the stock is officially available to be traded.

WHAT IS A STARTUP?

What comes to mind when you hear the term *startup*? You might think of Silicon Valley or tech companies like Netflix or Google. Those are good examples, although many startups exist outside the tech industry and the Silicon Valley area.

Basically, a startup is a young company that's formed by a handful of founders who have a business idea that is creative and new. They start off very small with just enough employees to test out the product and business model. The hope is that customers will embrace the new business idea and the startup will continue to grow.

A startup company tries to solve a problem or fulfill a need that's not currently being met by other companies (see the "bug list" on page 10 in chapter 1). Many startups are built around new technologies and try to be socially conscious. For example, a startup might try to find new forms of transportation that are cheaper and better for the environment.

Since startups are young companies, they usually need help to build their business. This is where venture capital firms (VCs) come in to lend money, resources, and expertise. Working at a startup can be exciting but also stressful. There's no guarantee that the business will be successful, and many startups go out of business. Some successful startups get bought by bigger companies or become public companies through the IPO process (see "In the Vault: Taking It Public" on page 84).

Here are some popular companies that began as startups:

- Uber
- Airbnb
- Instagram
- Snapchat
- YouTube

Fun fact: We worked at several startups over the years. Allison was a project manager at ZINIO (digital magazines) and StubHub (ticket sales). I did marketing for Lumosity (brain games) and Basis (fitness watches). Maybe one day you'll work at a startup (or start one)!

HISTORICAL NOTES: STARTUP FAILS

When most people think about startups, they think about all the really successful ones. Unfortunately, most startups don't do nearly as well as Instagram, which is why investing in them is so risky. Here are just a few examples of some of the biggest and costliest startup failures:

- **Munchery** had $117 million in funding but closed its doors due to too much competition in the food delivery space. It was in business from 2010 to 2019.
- **Jawbone,** which sold fitness trackers, headsets, and wireless speakers, was one of the costliest startup

failures of all time. The company was in business for 17 years and had almost $1 billion in funding ($930 million).

⇨ **Pets.com** was a very famous startup from the dot-com bust of 2001. It couldn't find a profitable way to ship heavy bags of pet food and litter. In the end, its most memorable product was a sock puppet from its TV commercials.

REAL ESTATE, ART, AND COLLECTIBLES

Another type of investing is buying physical assets like real estate, art, and collectibles.

The most common physical asset that people invest in is real estate. When you buy a house, you want a nice place to live, but you also hope it *appreciates* (increases) in value. When this happens, your *equity* (the value of the house minus the mortgage loan) goes up. For example, if your house is valued at $200,000 and the mortgage loan is $150,000, then your equity is $50,000 ($200,000 - $150,000 = $50,000).

You can also invest in *rental property*. This is when you buy a house or apartment building and rent it to tenants. You not only earn equity when the value goes up, but you also can make money from the rent.

Other assets you can invest in are art and collectibles. Some people buy art just because they love the beauty of it. But art can be an investment if the price appreciates. (Although it cannot be purchased, the *Mona Lisa* is estimated to be worth almost $1 billion!) Collectibles are collections of rare or unique items that can go up in value over time. Baseball cards, comic books, stamps, and coins are examples of things that people may collect.

Just be aware that not all physical assets are investments. For example, when you buy a brand-new car, it *depreciates* (goes down in value) as soon as you drive it off the car lot.

HISTORICAL NOTES:
FAMOUS COLLECTIBLES

I f you're wondering how expensive collectibles can be, just take a look at the record price paid for these items:

- ⇨ **Comic book:** $3.2 million for *Action Comics* #1 (first appearance of Superman)
- ⇨ **Baseball card:** $3.12 million for a 1909 Honus Wagner
- ⇨ **Football card:** $240,000 for a 1935 Bronko Nagurski
- ⇨ **Stamp:** 9 million euros ($10.16 million) for a British Guiana 1c Magenta
- ⇨ **Coin:** $10 million for a 1794 Flowing Hair silver/copper dollar
- ⇨ **Painting:** $450 million for Leonardo da Vinci's *Salvator Mundi*
- ⇨ **House:** $239.9 million for a New York City penthouse on Central Park South

You may never own any of these rare artifacts, but maybe you'll come across another unique collectible that will appreciate nicely for you.

Angel Investing

One of the highest-risk, highest-reward types of investing is called *angel investing*. What do you think of when you think of an angel? You probably think about a powerful being with wings, a harp, and a halo over their head. They come down from heaven to watch out for you and help you when you're in trouble.

That's kind of what an angel investor does, but they don't have wings. They watch over, help, and guide young entrepreneurs with their early stage startups. It's very similar to venture capital (VC) investing, but there are a few differences.

⇨ **Who invests:** VCs don't use their own money. Instead, they collect money from an investment company. Angel investors are usually wealthy individuals who invest their own money.

⇨ **When they invest:** VCs usually invest in companies that are a little bit more established. Angels invest in very early stage startups. These are young companies that are still trying to prove their business model.

⇨ **Investment amounts:** VCs usually invest several million dollars at a time. Since angels are using their own money and taking a bigger risk, they usually only invest a few hundred thousand dollars at a time. That's still a lot of money to risk!

Angel investors hope to make at least 20% to 25% on their investments. Sometimes they make much more than this, but sometimes they don't make anything at all.

RANK THE INVESTMENT LEVEL

The Dollar Duo would like to make some investments, but they don't know as much about risk and reward as you do. Can you help them assess the following investments?

Rank the following investments from 1 (lowest risk/reward) to 6 (highest risk/reward). You can go back and look at the descriptions on pages 53 and 67 to help.

⇨ **CD (certificate of deposit)**
⇨ **Stock of a new IPO company**
⇨ **Stock of an established 100-year-old company**
⇨ **Treasury bill (T-bill)**
⇨ **Highly rated (or junk) bond**
⇨ **Lottery ticket**

Once you have ranked the choices and helped the Dollar Duo make their investment decisions, you can see the correct rankings at the bottom of the page:

1: Treasury bill, 2: CD, 3: Highly rated (or junk) bond, 4: Stock of established company, 5: Stock of new company, 6: Lottery ticket

In order to be successful, angel investors have to do a lot of research. After they invest, they usually have to spend a lot of time with the young companies to provide expertise and advice.

TAKING STOCK

In chapter 5, you learned all about the fun world of high-risk/high-reward investments. Here are some things to remember:

☑ The financial world likes to use animals as symbols to describe the market: bears, bulls, and black swans, oh my! (See pages 70 to 72.)

☑ Angel investing is not about buying halos and wings. It's when a wealthy individual investor puts money into a very early stage company to help it get started (see page 90).

☑ You now know how to buy your first stock! You open up an account at an investment brokerage (like Vanguard, Fidelity, or Charles Schwab), do your research, and purchase individual stocks or stock funds right online (see page 75).

CHAPTER 6

Diversify Your Investments

N ow that you know the differences between low-risk and high-risk investments, how do you tell which investments are best for *you*? A strategy that smart investors use is called *diversification*.

You have probably heard the phrase "Don't put all your eggs in one basket." It dates back to the 17th century and refers to farmers gathering eggs from their hens. If they put them all in one basket and accidentally dropped that basket, they would lose all of their prized eggs! But if they spread the eggs out between several baskets and only dropped one of them, they would still have the eggs from the other baskets. *Whew!*

That's the idea behind diversifying your investments. You put a little money here and a little there, so if one type of investment does poorly, you still have money in other investments. We'll talk about ways to do that, like buying *funds* that have a whole bunch of stocks and/or bonds in one investment, in the pages that follow.

What Is Diversification?

Believe it or not, you can learn a valuable lesson about investing from a famous fairy tale. Do you remember the story of *Goldilocks and the Three Bears*? When Goldilocks tried the porridge, Papa Bear's was too hot and Mama Bear's was too cold, but Baby Bear's was *just right*.

What does this have to do with investing? Well, when you're investing, you don't want to be too low or too high when it comes to the risk and reward. You want to find that nice Baby Bear sweet spot that is *just right*.

How do you find that sweet spot when investing? It all comes down to *diversification* (not putting all your eggs in one basket). The way to do this is to look at your **asset allocation**. Asset *what*? This means examining how much you have invested in different types of investments.

To determine a good asset allocation, you can consider several factors: your age, your risk tolerance, and how long you have until you retire (or need to access that money). The most important factor is your age. The younger you are, the more you can invest in high-risk/high-reward investments because you have longer to recover from the downturns.

One way to calculate this is by using this formula:

100 – your age = % of stocks to own

The rest would be in bonds (and/or other low-risk investments).

Let's look at some examples of this rule. If you're currently 10 years old, you could invest 90% in high-risk stocks (100 – 10 = 90) and 10% in bonds and low-risk investments. When you're 50, you would invest 50% in stocks and 50% in bonds. (And, yes, when you're 100 years old, that means you would invest 100% in bonds and low-risk investments!)

Here's how those asset allocations would look in pie charts. If these were pizza pies, then you would get one slice of bonds at 10 years old and half of a pizza of bonds at 50 years old.

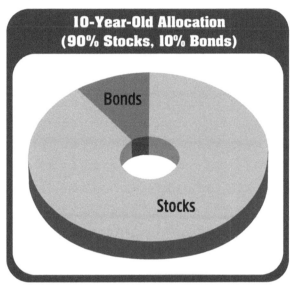

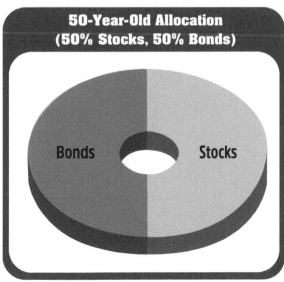

Wait, you're not done diversifying yet! We need to also make sure that your investment of 90% stock is also diversified. You do that by buying stock in a wide variety of companies and industries. If you bought only one company's stock, you would be putting 90% of all your money into that one basket!

A really easy way to do this is to buy an **index fund**. Remember back in chapter 5 when we talked about stock indexes like the S&P 500 (see page 69)? Well, you can buy a fund that covers all 500 of those stocks. That's a lot of different eggs in a lot of baskets!

This is sometimes called *passive investing* as opposed to *active investing*. When you constantly buy and sell specific company stocks, you are actively investing. On the other hand, passive investing is when you buy a diversified fund of stocks and/or bonds and hold on to them for a long time as they increase in value. This is also called the *buy and hold strategy*, and it's a very popular way to invest. Even Warren Buffett recommends this approach for most investors.

MIX AND MATCH

The Dollar Duo is here with another challenge: Find publicly traded companies that match your interests. This can be a good way to start thinking about which companies you might want to invest in.

1. Make a list of 5 to 10 of your interests or hobbies. Start by thinking of all the things you love to do. For example, your list might include bicycles, video games, comic books, and board games.

2. Find companies that are publicly traded to match each interest or hobby. Let's say you find two bicycle companies named Big Wheelz (BWZ) and Rough Tracks (RT). You would do a search for their *stock ticker symbols* to see if they are publicly traded.

Once you have a list of publicly traded companies that match your interests, then you can do some research on those companies and see if you would want to invest in any of them.

Exchange-Traded Funds

After reading about diversification and index funds, you may be thinking, *That sounds great, but how do I buy those kinds of funds?*

One of the easiest ways is to invest in what are called exchange-traded funds (or ETFs for short). ETFs are collections of stocks, bonds, and/or other investment types that you can buy just like you buy an individual company stock.

So, for example, if you wanted to invest in all of the stocks of the S&P 500, you wouldn't have to buy all of those stocks individually. That would be a lot of work! Instead, you could just purchase an S&P 500 ETF.

The cool thing is that ETFs come in all shapes and sizes, such as stocks, bonds, sectors (or industries), and commodities (like precious metals). Here are some of the investments you can make in each ETF:

- **Stock ETFs:** S&P 500, Russell 2000 (top 2000 small business stocks), Nasdaq 100 (top 100 technology stocks)
- **Bond ETFs:** Government, corporate, municipal, highly rated, high yield
- **Sector ETFs:** Biotech, energy, financial services, **Real Estate Investment Trust (REIT)**
- **Commodity ETFs:** Oil, natural gas, gold, silver

You can see from this selection of ETFs that it would be fairly easy to diversify your investments with these funds. And it's easy to invest in ETFs. You can research them just like you would individual company stocks, and you can buy them in your brokerage account. As always, just make sure to have an adult help and supervise your investments.

FACE VALUE: JOHN "JACK" BOGLE

John "Jack" Bogle (1929–2019) was a famous investor, businessman, and philanthropist. In 1974, he founded The Vanguard Group, which ultimately became the largest provider of mutual funds and the second-largest provider of ETFs in the financial world. In 1999, *Forbes* called him "one of the four investment giants of the 20th century."

Remember *index funds*? (See page 98.) Jack Bogle was the one who created the very first index fund! These funds changed the way personal investors could easily diversify their investments. Paul Samuelson, a Nobel Prize–winning economist, compared the creation of index funds to "the invention of the wheel, the alphabet, and Gutenberg printing."

Bogle's philosophy at Vanguard was to provide investors with low-cost investment options. He believed in investing for the long term using **dollar cost averaging** (an investing strategy where you divide your total investment into smaller periodic investments) and reinvesting dividends. His ideal investment was a low-cost index fund held for the investor's lifetime. Followers of John Bogle's strategy are called "Bogleheads."

Mutual Funds

Another way to buy a wide variety of investments at one time is with mutual funds. Similar to ETFs, mutual funds allow you to buy a collection of stocks, bonds, and/or other investments with one purchase.

You may be wondering, *So, what's the difference between mutual funds and ETFs?* That's a good question, because they are very similar types of investments. The main difference is that ETFs are *passively managed* and mutual funds are *actively managed* by a fund manager.

ETFs are just set to track a particular index (like the S&P 500) or sector (like oil and gas), so they don't need a professional fund manager to make any decisions. Mutual funds, on the other hand, use managers to make decisions about what investments are being bought and sold in the fund.

That means you pay slightly higher fees and expense ratios with mutual funds because you're paying an expert to make the decisions. This may sound like a bad idea because why would you want to pay more of your hard-earned money? Let's look at this a little closer. Sometimes mutual funds can perform well enough to do better than ETFs even after the higher fees. This is why it's important to do your research.

One type of mutual fund that can be helpful for new investors are *target retirement funds*. You select the year that you think you will retire, and the fund automatically sets and updates an appropriate asset allocation for your age. It's an easy way to diversify with the right mix of stocks and bonds if you're okay with paying a little more in management fees.

DIVERSIFY!

The Dollar Duo needs your help! They want to diversify their investments but aren't sure how.

Let's help them come up with a good plan, starting with the right asset allocation. Remember the formula to determine the percent of stock to own:

100 – your age = percent of stock to own

If the Dollar Duo are each 30 years old, then their asset allocation would be 70% stock and 30% bonds (and other low-risk investments).

If they have $1,000 to invest, that would be $700 for stock investments and $300 for bond and low-risk investments.

Here are the options they are considering. How much would you invest in each of these categories to ensure that they have the right allocation? Show your guardian to see if they would agree.

Stocks ($700 total):

⇨ **Individual company stocks = $ _____**
⇨ **S&P 500 index fund = $ _____**
⇨ **2050 target retirement fund = $ _____**

Bonds and low-risk investments ($300 total):

⇨ **Online savings account = $ _____**
⇨ **T-bills = $ _____**
⇨ **High-yield bonds = $ _____**

How would you like to retire in your 30s or 40s so you can travel, have adventures, and work on fun projects for the rest of your life? That is the idea behind a movement called *FIRE* (Financial Independence/Retiring Early).

The FIRE movement started becoming popular in the 2010s as more and more people realized they didn't want to work in stressful jobs for the rest of their lives. Allison and I were able to achieve FIRE in our 40s in 2015, and now we get to travel the world and write books!

The goal is to save and invest at least 25 times your yearly expenses. So if your yearly expenses are $50,000, then you would need to have $1,250,000 in savings and investments.

That seems like a lot (and it is); however, if you start investing wisely at an early age (like you will be able to after you read this book), you can easily get there. It also helps if you can *live frugally*, which means being smart about how you spend your money.

TAKING STOCK

In chapter 6, we explored why diversifying your investments is so important. Here are some things to remember:

☑ Being diversified in your investments is like making sure you don't put all your eggs in one basket (see page 96).

☑ ETFs are an easy way to buy an entire stock index or sector of the economy (see page 100).

☑ Mutual funds are like ETFs, but you have to pay a little extra because they're professionally managed (see page 102).

CHAPTER 7

Grow Your Money

A fter reading the previous six chapters, you now know more about investing than most kids your age (and many adults)! In this final chapter, we'll show you how to put everything you learned into practice—both now and in the future.

We'll look at how your life's journey may unfold when you start saving, investing, and growing your money at a young age. We'll start with the things you can do right away, like earning extra money, opening up a savings account, and following the stock market.

As you get older, your goal might be to buy a car, go to college, or start a business. Later in life you may want to buy a house or help your kids go to college. You might even want to retire early like we did! Investing when you're young can help you achieve those dreams and more.

What Now?

Successful people (especially investors) always set goals for themselves. Think of setting your investment goals like going on a road trip. If you don't know where you want to end up, it's hard to get there. You would end up driving in circles or even running into a roadblock. However, if you know where you want to end up (your goal), then you can create a road map to get there, safely and efficiently.

Even though you're young, there are many things you can do now to get a head start on your investing future. Let's start with the next few years. You can set goals to earn money, save money, and research investments.

Your goal should have a specific number or dollar amount, and it should have a time frame. Once you set your goal, you should then create specific steps to achieve that goal. You are more likely to achieve a difficult goal if you can break it down into several easier parts.

Here is an example: Say you want to create a goal around earning money. You could make your goal to earn $500 in the next 12 months. This is a specific amount of money and a defined time frame to make it happen. Once you have your goal, it's time to outline the steps to get there:

Step 1. Come up with ideas to earn money. Make a list of all the different ways you might be able to earn some extra cash. A great way to earn money is to offer a service. Services can be things like walking dogs, babysitting, mowing lawns, or running errands.

Step 2. Find customers. The best customers for your services are the people who live near you or whom you interact with regularly. Maybe your neighbors are physically unable to do certain things, or they are just too busy. They could really use your help.

Step 3. Market your services. Explain to your prospective customers what service you could provide to them. Tell them why you would do a good job (you love dogs or you used to babysit your little brother all the time). Suggest a fair fee for your services.

Step 4. Make your customer happy. Always do a good job and thank them for the opportunity. This will keep them coming back to hire you again, either for the same job or for other jobs.

Step 5. Ask for referrals. Once you've made your customer happy, ask them if they would refer you to their friends and relatives. This is called *word-of-mouth* advertising. Your clients are literally telling others they should hire you.

You can do the same goal-setting plan for saving money and researching investments.

FACE VALUE: MARK CUBAN

Y ou might know Mark Cuban as the owner of the NBA's Dallas Mavericks. He purchased the team in 2000 for $280 million, and in 2019 it was worth $2.25 billion. Or perhaps you know him from the ABC TV show *Shark Tank*. (From 2011 to 2020, he's invested $20 million in over 80 small businesses.)

Cuban, whose estimated net worth was $4.3 billion in 2019, has always been an entrepreneur. His philosophy is to look for needs and fill them before anyone else can. When he was 12 years old, he sold garbage bags to neighbors for $6 a pack. At 16, when the local newspaper went on strike, Cuban actually drove to Cleveland, Ohio, and bought newspapers to sell in Pittsburgh, Pennsylvania. That's over 250 miles roundtrip!

In the late 1980s, Cuban started a company called MicroSolutions, which he sold in 1990 for $6 million. He later created an online service that streamed sports events that was acquired by Yahoo in 1999 for $5.7 billion!

Dream Big

Getting started with earning money and saving money are the first steps on your financial journey. These are the building blocks of becoming a successful investor.

It may seem like the amount that you have saved to invest is very small right now. Don't be discouraged by that! Your main goal right now is simply to learn the basics of investing. Remember that compound interest will help your savings grow over long periods of time.

One question you may be asking is *Can I spend any of the money I'm saving, or do I just have to invest it all for the future?* Well, one of the nice things about building wealth is being able to enjoy it from time to time. This is why setting financial goals is so important. One good strategy is to set goals for different stages of your life. Those goals might include how much you want to earn, how much you want to save, and what big dreams you want to accomplish along the way.

How do you know if you can afford these big dreams? Figure out what the cost would be and then work backward. Use the same goal-setting strategy about earning money that we used in the last section (see page 108). Write out the step-by-step strategy so that you can be successful in achieving your financial goals and dreams.

Now, let's have some fun and think about big dreams you might have at different stages in life. Everyone's dreams are different. One person might want a big mansion and a fancy sports car, while the next person may prefer to spend their money on traveling around the world.

We'll start with your teen years. You may be interested in items like video games, bicycles, sporting goods, computers, and even your first car. There are also all kinds of fun and exciting experiences you could enjoy, like concerts, road trips, and sporting events. And don't forget about saving for your college tuition!

In your 20s and 30s, you'll have different goals. For example, you'll want your own apartment or house, some nice furniture, and maybe a better car. If you get married, you may be planning a nice wedding and honeymoon. This is also a great time to start traveling more and exploring the world.

If you start investing now, then in your 40s and 50s, you should be in a very nice financial situation for yourself and your family. You can upgrade your living situation to a nicer house if you want. You could travel even more. Allison and I have been to 30 countries so far, and we plan to get to 60 by the time we're 60 years old!

When you're 60 or older, if you have invested wisely, you will be in a great position to enjoy the rest of your life however you see fit because money will not be an issue.

LOOK INTO A CRYSTAL BALL

The Dollar Duo believes it's good to have goals in life. They want you to think about where you will be at age 20, 30, 40, and 50. Here are the different categories:

⇨ **Where** do you want to live? It could be another country, a different city or state, by the ocean, in the mountains, maybe even in outer space!

⇨ **What** do you want to be? Engineer, musician, CEO, politician, adventure tour guide, entrepreneur, etc.

⇨ **Whom** do you want to live with? Spouse, kids, roommates, friends, etc.

⇨ **What** hobbies do you want to have? Scuba diving, traveling, playing sports, writing, etc.

Fill out the table with where you see yourself at each of these ages. We won't hold you to these goals, so let your imagination run wild!

Age	Where	What	Who	Hobbies
20				
30				
40				
50				

Adulting

If the idea of investing right now seems difficult, don't worry! When you turn 18 years old and officially become an adult, it will be much easier.

First, you won't need adult supervision to open accounts and make investment decisions. Just make sure you still always do your research. Once you have a regular job, you will probably have a steady source of income. You can set aside part of this income for saving and investing on a regular basis.

One of the most common ways for many people to start investing is through their company's **401(k) plan** (see "What Are Retirement Funds?" on page 115). Your employer may automatically invest a small percentage of your income for you. You may not even notice that your paycheck is smaller, but as it grows and compounds over time, you'll be happy with the results. Sometimes your employer even matches some of the investment, meaning the company invests the same amount as you do (it's *free money*!).

When you are older, you can also try some investments that are higher risk and higher reward, such as investing in rental properties or starting your own business. You may want to start an online comic book store or set up an automobile repair shop in your neighborhood—dream big!

Starting your own business is like *investing in yourself*. You're taking a chance that your knowledge, research, and hard work will pay off with a profitable business. The nice thing is that in your 20s and 30s, you have time to recover if an investment doesn't work out well.

How do people know if they have enough money saved up to retire? It turns out there are a couple of "rules" you can follow.

The first is called the "4% Rule." It states that if you withdraw 4% or less per year of your **nest egg** (how much you have saved) for your expenses, then your money will probably not run out. For example, let's say you end up with $1 million at the age of 45 from all your saving and investing. That is enough to retire on if your yearly expenses are $40,000 or less (4% of $1 million).

Another way to look at it is the "Multiply by 25 Rule," which says that your nest egg should be at least 25 times your yearly expenses. If your expenses are $50,000, then your goal should be to have saved at least $1,250,000 (25 × $50,000).

What Are Retirement Funds?

IRA, 401(k), SEP, 403(b)—these are not new droids from the *Star Wars* movie franchise but different types of *retirement accounts*.

Retirement accounts are programs that make it easier to make investments for your future. The most common ones are 401(k) and IRA accounts. The investments can go into stocks, bonds, ETFs, or mutual funds.

The 401(k) plan is set up by your employer. You set a small percentage of your paycheck to be invested automatically for you. An Individual Retirement Account (IRA) is similar, but you contribute to this account on your own. Retirement accounts are either *traditional* or *Roth*. The difference is when you pay **taxes** on the money.

There are some rules for these accounts. For example, you have to wait until you are 59½ years old to take money out (otherwise there is a 10% penalty). So why do it? Because it makes investing much easier and lets you use compounding to work for you. The nice thing about these plans is that once you set them up, they work on autopilot. Investors refer to this as "set it and forget it."

READY, SET, FIRE!

The Dollar Duo wants to help you achieve FIRE by age 45. Imagine that you have $1.5 million saved up by then. Using the 4% Rule, you can withdraw $60,000 per year safely (or $5,000 per month).

This game will help you budget your money. If you want to retire early, you may have to reduce your spending in certain areas.

Here are the rules:

1. You can only pick one option from each category: housing, transportation, food, and entertainment.

2. Your total expense has to be $5,000 or less.

Now, see what choices you have to make to achieve FIRE. *Ready, set, go!*

Housing	Transportation	Food	Entertainment
House: $2,500	SUV: $2,000	Restaurants: $1,500	Travel: $500
Condo: $2,000	Electric car: $1,000	50/50 Restaurants/ Cooking: $1,000	Events (Concerts, Shows, Sports): $300
Apartment: $1,500	Scooter: $50	Cooking: $500	Movies: $100

When You're 60

After learning about all the different ways you can invest your money, you may be wondering what the ultimate goal is. Well, that all depends on *you*. Everyone is different, and each person has their own life goals.

Think about all the things you may want to accomplish in your life. While money can't buy happiness, it can provide you and your loved ones with a more comfortable and enjoyable lifestyle. Just for fun, let's take out our crystal ball and try to look into your future.

Do you want to send your kids to college without needing loans? There is an investment program called a 529 plan that helps you save for your children's education. It works like a 401(k) plan by allowing you to invest money *tax-deferred* (meaning you pay taxes on it later). Providing an education is one of the best gifts you can offer your loved ones. Allison's parents were able to save enough to send her to college, which helped prepare her for much of the success she's had in life.

Do you want to retire young? While most people think about waiting until they are 65 to retire, perhaps you can retire at 55. Or maybe you can even retire by 45 like we did. If you start saving and investing when you're young, you have a great opportunity to become financially independent at an early age. This would provide you with the freedom to pursue whatever exciting dreams and adventures you can imagine. Maybe you want to buy an RV and travel to every state in the country. Or you want to visit 60 countries by the time you're 60 years old (that's our goal!).

Do you want to help make the world a better place? We've talked about some of the many ways you can make a difference. For example, you can invest in companies that are green or that are owned by women or minorities. You can also make an impact by donating your time and resources to causes that are meaningful to you.

All of this is possible if you save and invest. You don't have to be a financial analyst or economist to be a smart investor. Here are some celebrities from TV, movies, and music who have made wise investments to increase their wealth:

⇨ **Ashton Kutcher:** Silicon Valley investments

⇨ **Jared Leto:** Coffee, mattresses, tech companies

⇨ **John Legend:** Clothing, online retail, water filtration

⇨ **Reese Witherspoon:** Production company, clothing line

⇨ **Arnold Schwarzenegger:** Real estate, restaurants, investment firm

⇨ **Jessica Alba:** Household goods, body care products

It takes hard work and effort, but if you apply what you learned in this book, you will be in good shape financially. As they say in the fairy tales, ". . . and you'll live happily ever after!"

YOUR MONEY'S WORTH: THE FUTURE

In this chapter, you've set goals and imagined what your life might be like until you're 60 years old. Now imagine you're at your 90th birthday party! What will your friends and family say about how you lived your life?

This is called your *legacy*. It's how you wish to be remembered and what you leave behind for future generations. Perhaps you'll be remembered as a great leader, an adventurer, an innovator, or an artist.

Here are some of the ways you could leave your mark:

⇨ **Work:** Being a leader and pioneer in your field
⇨ **Philanthropy:** Volunteering, donating to charities and causes you believe in, mentoring young people
⇨ **Creativity:** Putting new things out into the world (like art, books, and businesses)

You can even set up your own charitable foundation later in life to provide grants, endowments, and scholarships. This is one way the money you've earned over the years can have a lasting impact.

TEST YOUR KNOW-HOW

For your last activity, the Dollar Duo wants to see how much you've learned:

1. Where were the first coins from?
  A. Lydia
  B. London
  C. Libya

2. What is the formula for compound interest?
  A. $P \times (1 + n)^i$
  B. $N \times (1 + i)^p$
  C. $P \times (1 + i)^n$

3. What should *not* be used for investing research?
  A. Earnings growth
  B. Your intuition
  C. Stability

4. What is true of a highly rated bond?
  A. Rated BB or lower
  B. Less risky than a high-yield bond
  C. Sometimes called "non-investment grade"

Don't worry if you missed some. Investing is a lifelong learning process!

5. Which of these investments has the highest risk?
  A. Junk bond
  B. S&P 500 index fund
  C. Startup

6. What does ETF stand for?
  A. Exchange-traded fund
  B. Easily traded fund
  C. Exchange-transferred fund

7. What is *not* true of a 401(k) plan?
  A. Offers tax advantages
  B. Administered by your employer
  C. Can be withdrawn with no penalty at any time

Answers: 1. A, 2. C, 3. B, 4. B, 5. C, 6. A, 7. C

TAKING STOCK

In chapter 7, we looked at how saving and investing will help you throughout your life. Here are some things to remember:

☑ You can create a step-by-step plan for achieving your money goals (see page 108).

☑ It's okay to have big dreams for what you want to accomplish at each stage of life (see page 110).

☑ Starting to invest when you're young will help you create the life you want and live happily ever after! (See page 117.)

Glossary

401(k): A plan set up by your employer that allows you to transfer money from your paycheck into an investment account

asset: Something of value (like cash, stocks, or property) that can be used to build wealth or pay down debt

asset allocation: An investment strategy that balances risk and reward by dividing an investor's assets (or investments) into different types of investments, such as stocks and bonds

bankruptcy: This is a legal process used by people or companies who cannot repay their debts. It is typically imposed by a court order and is used to seek relief from some or all of the debt.

brokerage firm: An institution that allows people to buy and sell financial products like stocks, bonds, mutual funds, and exchange-traded funds (ETFs)

certificate of deposit (CD): A financial product sold by banks and credit unions that has a specific time frame and usually a fixed interest rate

credit union: A bank for specific groups, such as teachers or members of the military

dollar cost averaging: This is a strategy where an investor divides up the total amount of their investment across periodic purchases of an asset (like weekly or monthly). The goal is to purchase the asset at different price points to avoid trying to "time the market."

earnings: The after-tax net income for a company (sometimes referred to as the "bottom line")

expense ratio: The percentage of a fund's assets that are used to pay for expenses, like administrative, management, and advertising costs

Federal Reserve (Fed): The central banking system of the United States, created in 1913, which manages the nation's monetary policy and oversees banking regulations

gross domestic product (GDP): The monetary value of all finished goods and services produced within a country during a specific period

index fund: A type of mutual fund or ETF that buys all the stock in a particular index, such as the 500 stocks in the S&P 500 or the 30 stocks tracked by the Dow Jones

interest: This is the cost of borrowing money. For savers, it's the amount your bank will pay you for lending them the money you are saving or investing.

investing: Putting money into something with the expectation that it will increase in value

liquidity: The ability to withdraw your money from an investment at any given time

maturity: The lifetime of an investment vehicle, such as a loan or Treasury bill

nest egg: The total amount of money and assets you have saved up

passive income: Earning money without having to actively generate it

principal: The amount of money you invest before earning interest

profitability: Income from a company's sales minus its costs

Real Estate Investment Trust (REIT): Sometimes called "real estate stocks," they are companies that own and manage real estate properties and mortgages.

return on investment (ROI): A measurement of how efficient an investment is; calculated by comparing the profit versus the cost of the investment

revenue: The income that a business makes from selling its products and services

stock indexes: They measure a subset of the stock market. Examples are the Dow Jones Industrial Average and the Nasdaq Composite.

stock shares: Units of stock, or ownership in a company

stocks: Portions of a corporation that give the stockholder part ownership of that company

taxes: Fees levied on individuals or companies from a government (local, state, or federal) to pay for government activities

yield: The earnings generated by an investment over a period of time

Resources

Here are some additional books you can read and some websites you can visit to learn more about investing, personal finance, and building wealth.

BOOKS

⇨ *The Millionaire Next Door: The Surprising Secrets of America's Wealthy* by Thomas J. Stanley and William D. Danko
This book identifies seven common traits that show up again and again among those who have accumulated wealth.

⇨ *The Richest Man in Babylon* by George S. Clason
This is one of the most inspirational works on the subject of thrift, financial planning, and personal wealth.

⇨ *The Simple Path to Wealth: Your Road Map to Financial Independence and a Rich, Free Life* by J. L. Collins
This book grew out of a series of letters to the author's daughter about money and investing.

WEBSITES

⇨ *Investopedia.com*
Provides investing and finance education along with reviews, ratings, and comparisons of various financial products such as brokerage accounts

➪ *Investor.gov*

Provides a free compound interest calculator so you can see how much your money can grow: Investor.gov /financial-tools-calculators/calculators/compound -interest-calculator

➪ *MarketWatch.com*

Provides financial information, business news, analysis, and stock market data

➪ *Yahoo! Finance (FinanceYahoo.com)*

Provides financial news, data, and commentary, including stock quotes, press releases, financial reports, and original content

Index

About the Authors

Dylin Redling and **Allison Tom** are a married couple living in Oakland, California. Their book *Start Your F.I.R.E. (Financial Independence Retire Early): A Modern Guide to Early Retirement* and their website RetireBy45.com provide inspiration and tips for achieving FIRE.

They have appeared in *Forbes, CNBC*, and many other publications. Prior to reaching FIRE in 2015, Dylin was an online marketing professional and Allison was a technical project manager.

Allison grew up in NYC and graduated from Dartmouth University. Dylin graduated from The Ohio State University.